Electronic Conveyancing:
A Practical Guide

AUSTRALIA
Law Book Co.
Sydney

CANADA and USA
Carswell
Toronto

HONG KONG
Sweet & Maxwell Asia

NEW ZEALAND
Brookers
Auckland

SINGAPORE and MALAYSIA
Sweet & Maxwell Asia
Singapore and Kuala Lumpur

Electronic Conveyancing: A Practical Guide

by

Paul Butt
College of Law, Chester

London
Sweet & Maxwell
2006

Published in 2006 by
Sweet & Maxwell Ltd,
100 Avenue Road
Swiss Cottage, London NW3 3PF
http://www.sweetandmaxwell.thomson.com

Typeset by J.P. Price, Chilcompton, Somerset
Printed in Great Britain by
Hobbs the Printers Ltd, Southampton, Hants

No natural forests were destroyed to make this product;
only farmed timber was used and replanted.

A CIP catalogue record for this book is available from the
British Library

ISBN 0 421 96500 2
978 0 421 96500 3

Contents

Chapter 4 — Getting Ready for E-Conveyancing

Chapter 5 — Will it work?

Chapter 1

Why E-Conveyancing?

INTRODUCTION

'It seems fairly certain now that a means of completing property transactions electronically . . . is inevitable.'

So said Barry Douse in July 2005; and he was speaking not of **1.01** England and Wales but of Australia. (Barry Douse is Executive Manager, Production and Business Development, in the Department of Land and Property Information in New South Wales.) The State of Victoria already has a pilot scheme ready to run and South Africa is not far behind. Ontario in Canada, Florida in the United States, and New Zealand are already operating a system of e-conveyancing, albeit on a smaller scale than will be required in England and Wales, or in Australia.

So it is not just England and Wales that are going down the **1.02** route to e-conveyancing. Other common law jurisdictions are going there also, and even going there first. Not being the first does, of course, have advantages in that we can learn from how others have (successfully) achieved e-conveyancing in a legal system similar to our own.

A survey of the other systems in use—just to show to the doubters that they are in use and that they do work, might be useful.

Canada

Canada is the world leader in electronic registration. In the **1.03** eighties an alliance between the Ontario Ministry of Consumer and Business Services and a private company called Teranet® led to the world's first remote electronic document land registration system being created. For the last 10 years the automated land registry system has meant that sellers and buyers can retrieve and access digital title documents needed for property transfers. Accredited lawyers and their agents create and submit the electronic title transfer documents, which then become the official record.

Central to the success has been the Province of Ontario Land Registration Information System—POLARIS®. Teranet has automated and electronically mapped some 3.2 million properties, while a huge database of some 125–150 million imaged documents which correlate to parcel data has been created.

1.04   Potential legal hurdles were overcome by the passing of innovative legislation that stipulates that electronic documents that create, transfer or otherwise dispose of an estate or interest in land are not required to be in writing or to be signed. The deed as a paper document effectively disappears and all that is submitted to the registrar is an electronic document authenticated by the digital signature of the presenting conveyancer.

In August 2005, Ontario reported that the five-millionth electronic transaction was successfully completed. The number of monthly electronic registrations is now, on average, running at 150,000 per month.

New Zealand

1.05   New Zealand has introduced a system that is similar to that in operation in Ontario. Called Landonline, it is a project initiated by Land Information New Zealand ("LINZ") that has converted millions of title records, title instruments, plans, parcels and geodetic survey marks into an electronic format. Ultimately, the entire conveyancing process will be automated, cutting the turnaround of lodgments from the present 10–15 days to 24 hours.

The project has been implemented in a phased roll-out schedule. Implementation has been so successful that the New Zealand Government has now set dates for the complete phasing out of paper-based conveyancing. It will be compulsory for all simple conveyancing and mortgage transactions by August 1, 2007 (i.e. next year!). It will be compulsory for all transactions by July 1, 2008.

United States of America—Florida

1.06   As long ago as July 2000 the first online mortgage application and paperless real estate "closing" took place in Florida. The transaction was then electronically recorded by the county, title insurance was issued, and images and index data for the deed and mortgage were digitally sealed before being transmitted to the Broward County Records Division through a website portal created especially for electronic transactions. Other United States jurisdictions are also proceeding towards the full implementation of electronic conveyancing.

Scotland

Even closer to home, Scotland has also initiated plans for **1.07**
e-conveyancing. The Automated Registration of Title to Land
("ARTL") project has been initiated. This aims to introduce
paper-free registration of title to rights in land. After a successful
pilot, the system will be rolled out. It is also proposed that ARTL
will only process routine dealings of whole registered interests in
land, such as either adding or removing entire entries in the
Proprietorship and Charges Sections of the title sheet.

Instead of preparing paper deeds and registration forms, all
applications will be completed online. The paper deed will be
replaced by a digital deed that will be created within the ARTL
system. This process will be completed using the Internet to
access the ARTL system and will result in the automatic updating
of the Land Register title sheet.

The Law Society of Scotland and the Council of Mortgage
Lenders support this initiative, as do the Scottish Executive Justice
Department, Ministers and the Scottish Consumers Council.

Ireland

In the Irish Republic, the Law Reform Commission published **1.08**
proposals in April 2006 aimed at developing a system of
electronic conveyancing in Ireland. This was stated to be
"particularly urgent".

England and Wales

In England and Wales the Labour Government was elected in **1.09**
1997 on a programme that included making increased use of internet technology to make Britain a "world leader" in electronic
commerce. There was a pledge to make all of "our laws and
rules" e-commerce friendly. This lead directly to the Electronic
Communications Act of 2000 which was designed to facilitate e-
commerce.

Government also pledged to allow access to all its services electronically so as to make access to public services more user
friendly and more cost effective. This has resulted, for example, in
tax payers being able to file income tax returns on line—and also
Land Transaction Returns on-line to assess liability to Stamp Duty
Land Tax.

As far as Conveyancing itself is concerned, the Law **1.10**
Commission and Land Registry joint consultation document
"Land Registration for the Twenty First Century" published in
1998 first set out preliminary proposals as to how e-conveyancing
might work in England and Wales. This was then followed in

November 2000 by the Government establishing a steering group to oversee the implementation of the proposals. It was then announced in the Queen's Speech in November 2001 that the Government would bring in legislation to make provision for e-conveyancing. There then followed the draft Land Registration Bill (to become the LRA 2002). This was to set the legislative framework for e-conveyancing and contained more details as to how the system might work. These have since evolved over the years following consultation with various "stakeholders".

1.11   Following consultation, the strategy for the implantation of e-conveyancing was approved by the Government in September 2003 (although it was not made public until November of that year). The strategy set out the system as it is at present being developed. The e-conveyancing service will, we were told, comprise three main elements:

- a central service (to be controlled by the Land Registry)

- an electronic funds transfer ("EFT") service

- a channel access service. This will provide a means of users being able to access and make use of the other two services. It was envisaged that the "channels" might well be operated by the private sector and could offer value added services.

1.12   The proposals were further defined in August 2004 and the Land Registry web site now carries a definitive document—"Defining the Service; E-conveyancing"—setting out how the service will work in practice.

But in all of this there does not seem to have been any rush of house buyers or other property owners demanding that e-conveyancing should be introduced—let alone conveyancers themselves.

WHAT ARE THE BENEFITS OF E-CONVEYANCING?

1.13   In December 2001, the then Lord Chancellor, Derry Irvine set out the Government's objectives in introducing e-conveyancing:

"The development of electronic conveyancing services will bring major benefits to both homebuyers and businesses in their dealings in land and property. They will make the property market more transparent and the property transaction process faster, cheaper and more efficient."

1.14   The Land Registry web site sets out a mission statement with regard to the introduction of e-conveyancing:

"Our mission is to 'make conveyancing easier for all'—
specifically, to develop an electronic system of conveyancing
that makes buying and selling houses easier for the general
public, conveyancing professionals, and other parties
involved in the process.

Our vision is to deliver a world-class conveyancing service,
where:

- the worry and risk of the conveyancing process are
  significantly reduced
- authorised parties involved in a conveyancing transaction
  can exchange information quickly, securely and reliably with
  each other and Land Registry
- registration will be confirmed immediately on completion
- up-to-date and accurate information is available on the progress of all linked conveyancing transactions
- funds can be transferred immediately, securely and reliably.

We aim to:

- transform the conveyancing service in England and Wales
  and safeguard fair competition
- improve the house-buying and selling process for the public
- deliver high-quality and accessible services
- run e-conveyancing efficiently and effectively
- support joined-up government
- deliver the e-conveyancing programme on time and within
  budget."

Very grand aims—but at least the Land Registry statement
omits the Lord Chancellor's reference to making conveyancing
"cheaper". And talking about making things cheaper, leads to
another question.

How much will it cost?

One of the (many) criticisms leveled at the whole idea of **1.15**
e-conveyancing, is how much setting up such a system will cost.
(See for example IT security expert Bob Browning at textor.com
and Raymond Perry in the Estates Gazette for September 18,
2003.)

And as they point out, the problem is that we just do not know
how much it will/has cost. And we are not talking about the cost
to the profession to put in place the systems and procedures to
enable it to function within an e-conveyancing environment, but
the cost to the public purse of all the work undertaken/yet to be
undertaken by the Land Registry; the cost of the research, the
consultation, the employment of outside specialist consultants,

creating computer systems, digital signatures, procedures for electronic funds transfers etc. It certainly will not have been cheap—and we are all paying for it.

1.16   However, in July 2005, when it was announced that the e-conveyancing pilot would take place in 2007 (now confirmed as October 2007), it was revealed that IBM had won the contract for overseeing the final stages of developing and building the IT that will support the system. This contract alone is reported to be worth £21 million over a five-year period.

Conclusion

1.17   In any event, whatever the cost, like it or not, the Government is set on introducing e-conveyancing. Just like Home Information Packs, too much Government time, effort and money has been expended for it now to go away, although many conveyancers may wish that both of these would do just that. So we must accept that it is on its way and ensure that we are ready and able to use it when it does arrive.

Chapter 2

How Will it Work?—Outline of a Typical E-Conveyancing Transaction

The Law Commission report in July 2001 introducing the Land **2.01** Registration Bill, that became the 2002 Act, was entitled "Land Registration for the Twenty First Century—A Conveyancing Revolution". This set out in some detail how a transfer of registered land might take place once e-conveyancing was in place. It was emphasised that these proposals were not cast in stone and were open to change in the light of experience. Both the Law Commission originally and the Land Registry subsequently have undertaken extensive consultation with conveyancers and others, both before and since the publication of the Bill, and some changes have been introduced to the proposed system as a result of these. However, the fundamental ideas set out in the Report seem likely to form the basis of the system when it is introduced.

The 2002 Act lays down the statutory foundations for e-conveyancing, providing for the new rules and procedures required, for example containing provisions enabling e-conveyancing to be made compulsory and providing for "network access agreements", allowing access without which a conveyancer will not be able to participate in e-conveyancing.

PROBLEMS WITH THE PRESENT SYSTEM

At the moment the contract and transfer in a sale of land are **2.02** paper documents. After completion the necessary forms have to be submitted to HM Revenue and Customs giving details of the transaction and paying any stamp duty land tax ("SDLT") necessary. This is necessary before registration in order to obtain an SDLT certificate without which registration cannot be effected. On receipt of this, the transfer is then submitted to the Land

Registry (along with a prescribed form of application, usually AP1), for registration to be effected. Although the purchaser does not become the legal owner unless, and until, he is registered, the effect of the contract is to give him an interest in equity over the land from that date.

There is thus an inevitable hiatus between the completion of the transaction in the solicitors' office and the actual registration of that transaction, and this has been a source of problems with regard to interests arising over the land between completion and the actual registration of that transaction.

2.03   Also a problem is the fact that the receipt of the application by the Land Registry is the first time that the Land Registry will have seen details of the transaction. If any problems are discovered by the Land Registry with regard to the documentation, then it will have to raise requisitions of the applicant to resolve these. There may well be some delay in resolving these as the applicant may have to go back to the seller in order to try and provide the answers requested. The seller may not be over-keen to co-operate, bearing in mind that he has already got his money, and there may be no contractual obligation for him to do so. Prior to the 2002 Act, it was apparently the case that "about 50 per cent" of applications were defective in some way, but this number has now fallen considerably following the introduction of new prescribed forms. But despite this possible delay, the application takes effect from the date upon which the application is deemed to be delivered to the Land Registry.

2.04   Also stated as a problem is the fact that the actual registration itself is conducted entirely by the staff of HM Land Registry: "The solicitor or licensed conveyancer who submits the application for registration has no part in that process." Whether many solicitors would see that as a problem is another matter! However, maybe the point is that if the solicitor had more involvement any apparent problems could be more easily resolved.

THE NEW SYSTEM IN OUTLINE

2.05   The e-conveyancing service will comprise three main elements:

- a central service
- an electronic funds transfer ("EFT") service
- a channel access service.

The central service will link all participants in a conveyancing transaction, co-ordinate the key milestones of contract exchange and completion, and update the register. To maintain the integrity of the register the central service will be managed and controlled by the Land Registry.

An EFT service will be linked to the central service. The central service will be responsible for processing and accounting for all monies involved in a transaction, and in a chain of transactions, whether on exchange or completion, and to settle associated costs—e.g. SDLT and Land Registry fees. The EFT service will then make the payments. It will enable payments to be made simultaneously and irrevocably, with greater efficiency and certainty than at present and, importantly, will enable buyers to know not only the day of completion but also the time when the keys to their new home will be released.

The channel access service will be developed to enable users to **2.06** access the above services. The Land Registry will develop and implement its own "single channel" in a "mixed economy" environment. This means that commercial providers, such as the National Land Information Service ("NLIS") channels, may provide access to e-conveyancing services, and large firms, or groups of firms, can also elect to build their own access if they so choose.

So in essence the idea behind the new system is very simple— everything will be done electronically. Title will be investigated on-line and searches made and results received in the same way. Of course, by the time we have e-conveyancing, Home Information Packs ("HIPs") will have become compulsory in residential transactions, but these will probably be available electronically. In any event in most cases it will be necessary for the buyer to conduct further searches as not all necessary searches will be included in the pack.

The contract will also be drafted as an electronic document and **2.07** submitted for approval electronically. But here will be a major change. The Land Registry will become involved at this stage, ensuring that there are no problems with the contract—problems that in the present system would not be discovered until an application for registration is made. The Land Registry will also have an involvement with regard to chains of transactions. There will be a "chain matrix" viewable on-line by all parties to the chain and designed to identify where and why delays are occurring along the chain. There will also be a Land Registry "chain manager" who will be responsible for identify delays and "encouraging" the "offending parties" to complete the steps necessary so that the chain can proceed. How sad that the Land Registry should chose such emotive wording as "offending party" with regard to someone not yet ready to proceed. The delay may well be completely outside their control! Much more will be said about the Chain Matrix below and at 5.34.

Exchange, completion and payment of monies would all be effected electronically. And here is the other major change. There will be no "registration gap". On completion, the register will automatically be changed by the action of the parties' conveyancers.

LAND REGISTRY DEMONSTRATION MODEL

2.08   A demonstration model showing how the e-conveyancing system might work in the context of a chain of transactions can be downloaded from the Land Registry web site. This is essential viewing and in particular clearly demonstrates how the Land Registry will be involved in the process almost from day one. It also clearly shows the working of the Chain Matrix.

HOW IT WILL WORK IN DETAIL

2.09   So how will a conveyancer handle a typical house purchase under the new system? Again, we will assume that the HIP system has also been introduced, although if common sense prevails and the system is scrapped, the changes will really only relate to the question as to whom undertakes the searches. The system of e-conveyancing will be based on a secure communications system (i.e. an intranet) accessible by "contractually authorised professionals" i.e. conveyancers, estate agents and mortgage lenders. The contractual authorisation will take the form of a Network Access Agreement. Only those solicitors or licensed conveyancers who have been authorised by the Land Registry to do so will be permitted to conduct e-conveyancing. The Registry will be obliged to contract with any solicitor or licensed conveyancer who meets the specified criteria. These specified criteria will be the subject of wide consultation and discussion with the relevant professional and other interested bodies.

The conveyancer will take instructions from the buyer and obtain identification evidence in the usual way. "In the usual way"—but increasingly as more clients and conveyancers get to use modern communications system to the full, this act of taking instructions will inevitably also be more often undertaken electronically via the conveyancer's website. But the point is that the same kind of information will be needed as under the present system.

2.10   The conveyancer will then have to confirm instructions and comply with the usual client care requirements—again, in the future this will increasingly be undertaken by email. Some conveyancers already communicate with clients by email. We are all going to have to get used to communicating that way—clients will expect it—and there will be no point in conducting the remainder of the transaction electronically if communication with the client is still to be undertaken by the old fashioned "snail mail", as the post is sometimes derisorily called.

As mentioned in the introduction, one of the more controversial features of e-conveyancing as it relates to residential transactions will be the introduction of the "chain matrix" and "chain manager". Once a conveyancer has been instructed to act in a residential transaction, he will be "required" to inform the chain manager of that fact. This requirement will be one of the terms of the Network Access Agreement, the ultimate sanction for non-compliance being the suspension of the agreement. However, as this would in effect mean that the conveyancer in question could then no longer conduct conveyancing work, this would only be likely in the most extreme situations.

There will be further requirements in the Network Access **2.11** Agreement for each conveyancer to provide information to the chain manager as to the completion of the various pre-contractual stages of the transaction, such as investigating title, carrying out local searches, obtaining mortgage offers, etc. This requirement will override the professional duties to the client of client confidentiality. The chain manager will then be able to build up a picture of the chain so that he can identify any persons in the chain who are delaying the process. This information will be made available via the secure Intranet to all parties in the chain. Although it is not anticipated that the chain manager will have any powers of compulsion as such, he will be able to "encourage the offending parties" to complete the steps that are still to be performed. One has to say how could there be any element of compulsion here—you cannot compel someone to be provided with a satisfactory mortgage offer. There will also inevitably be pressure from others in the chain who are ready to contract.

The Law Commission (and the Land Registry) consider that the **2.12** power to manage chains in this way to be an important feature of the proposals for e-conveyancing:

> "Chains are a major cause of disquiet in the conveyancing process, particularly in relation to domestic conveyancing. By providing a means of controlling and expediting chains, the Bill should do much to alleviate the frustrations that are suffered by so many buyers and sellers of land. It is anticipated that it should prevent chains from collapsing."

Well, it is certainly true that chains are a cause of disquiet, but whether a matrix can control and expedite the chain is another matter. This suggestion as to chain management has, perhaps, been the most criticised part of the proposals for e-conveyancing. It has obviously been designed by someone with no experience of everyday conveyancing practice. Further comments on the matrix and whether it will work will be made at 5.34.

2.13   The buyer's conveyancer will then peruse the HIP (just as now the pre-contract package of information provided by the seller's conveyancer would be considered.) The HIP will not contain a contract, but will contain official copy entries and copies of certain searches. What those searches will be will depend upon the pack provider but may well just consist of the local search and CON29 enquiries and the CON29DW drainage and water enquires. These are the only searches required to be included in the pack; any others are purely voluntary. The pack may be supplied electronically or may be a paper-based hard copy. The pack will no longer have to contain a Home Condition Report, i.e. a form of basic survey, although one may be included. It must, however, contain an Energy Performance Certificate stating how energy efficient the house is. Neither of these will be within the conveyancer's expertise to consider. Other forms may also be included—in particular the Fixtures, Fittings and Contents Form and the Property Information Form. These will need considering by the conveyancer in the same way as the present forms are.

2.14   At the outset at least, the buyer's conveyancer will therefore have the local search and drainage search, which will need studying as now—but the conveyancer will also have to consider the date that these searches were made—there will be no obligation on the seller to update the information contained in the pack. So if a house has been on the market for more than six months, it will be necessary for the buyer's conveyancer to obtain up to date searches to replace those in the pack. In addition, the conveyancer, as now, will need to consider what extra searches will need doing. Therefore, as now, mining or commons registration searches may be necessary, as will chancel repairs or environmental searches. The searches that will be required will be the same as now, as will the need to consider the results and advise the client as to their effect. The only difference that there will be at this stage will be how these searches are made. They will be made electronically using one of the NLIS channels and the results will come back electronically to your computer. Of course, a large number of firms are already making use of the NLIS system, so they will see little change.

2.15   Communications between the seller's and buyer's conveyancers will be electronic. So the buyer will confirm to the seller's that they have been instructed—and vice versa, but by email rather than by letter as may happen at the moment. And ultimately the buyer will receive from the seller the draft contract for the sale. This will not be a paper-based document but a computer file. Again, for many not a major change—many firms already draft contracts from computerised templates and then print off a hard copy. Under the new scheme it will be a copy of the electronic file which is sent to the other side. Assuming that the Fixtures, Fittings and Contents Form and Property Information Form were not provided in the HIP, the seller's conveyancer will also provide completed versions of these—again electronically. The buyer's conveyancer will, of course, have to study these documents and make any further enquiries or negotiate any amendments to the draft contract in exactly the same circumstances as now. But again enquiries/negotiations not made over the telephone, will be made electronically, not by a letter sent through the post.

Therefore, the basics in a conveyancing transaction will still be the same as today—it is just the way of carrying them out that will change. However, there will be one major difference at the draft contract stage. Remember the problems that might be caused because of the Land Registry only becoming involved after completion. The Law Commission report proposed that this could be solved by the approved draft contract being submitted to the Land Registry to be checked electronically to ensure that there were no discrepancies with the Register. The present proposals suggest that the Land Registry will become involved even earlier. When the draft contract is submitted by the seller to the buyer, automatic validation checks will compare contract data with Land Registry data and electronic messages will indicate any discrepancies and/ or omissions. At the same time, a new "notional" register will be built on the system indicating, as each document is prepared, what the new register would look like. **2.16**

Like many aspects of the proposals, it all sounds very good in theory. It remains to be seen whether the computerised checking system will be able to cope with the various ways in which conveyancers draft contracts. Presumably it will be able to pick up discrepancies in the names of the registered proprietors, or the address or title number of the property, but precisely what other problems with contracts it will be able to spot remains to be seen. If on a sale of part it could check whether the correct easements and covenants had been granted and reserved, then it might be something worth having, but one fears that like many computerised systems it will merely generate a number of imagined problems, thus causing more work than it saves. The danger is that the buyer's conveyancer will think that as this Land Registry check has not spotted any problems, then the contract must be in order and no further checking by the buyer is needed. **2.17**

Moving back to how our transaction might progress, the conveyancers involved will have the same matters to deal with as in any other transaction. So checking the results of searches, checking finances, etc, will still be the order of the day. But assuming that everything is in order, we come to the usual practice of exchange. Contracts will still need signing and exchanging, deposits will still need obtaining from the client and paying over to the seller. Completion dates will still need agreeing and synchronising along the chain. Contracts will still need exchanging on all transactions in the chain or none at all. Arranging all this is **2.18** sometimes a conveyancers worst nightmare and here the electronic system will be a big help.

Contracts will be signed and exchanged electronically and deposits will be transferred in the same way. The methods of Electronic Fund Transfer and electronic signatures proposed will be looked at separately (see 2.29 and 2.36), but we can now consider how the mechanics of exchanging will be improved under the new system.

2.19   As stated, in a dependent sale and purchase, the conveyancer must ensure that the completion dates agreed for both are the same. Equally, he must ensure that either both contracts are exchanged or neither is. The client must not be left in a situation that he has contracted to sell his existing property, but has no house to move into, or that he has contracted to buy the new house, but cannot afford to proceed because he has not sold his existing property. And, of course, every other conveyancer acting for the other "links in the chain" has the same worries. And if it is not achieved, if the sale is agreed without the purchase, or vice versa, the conveyancer has been negligent.

And the same applies with regard to completion. All the dates for all the transactions along the chain must be the same. This synchronisation of the exchanges, and agreeing the same completion date on every link in the chain, is the single most difficult aspect of modern day conveyancing. The fact that it is achieved is a great tribute to those involved in the process and is much under-appreciated by the public and Government alike.

2.20   The other practical problem—again under appreciated by clients—is the problem of everyone wanting to use the deposit received on their sale as the deposit on their purchase. This often means that a deposit paid by a first time buyer has to be passed along the chain from buyer to seller. This can be very difficult to achieve, even using the clearing banks' modern computerised systems. Only so many money transfers can be handled in one day. (The same problem with passing on the money also arises on completion, when the completion monies have to be passed along the chain on the agreed completion day.) Usually it all works fine, but any delay along the chain and the transaction at the end may be in difficulty.

2.21   Help in achieving this will be much appreciated by conveyancers. So how will the electronic system help? Well, everything will take place electronically. Exchange and transfer of money all along the chain will take place will take place simultaneously.

"Contracts will be exchanged electronically when the buyer's and seller's conveyancers have signalled that agreement has been reached and contracts have been signed and released for electronic exchange. The central service will provide for automatic exchange of contracts relating to all transactions in a property chain."

Equally the electronic funds transfer system will provide for the deposit money to be paid automatically to the ultimate recipient or recipients.

As far as agreeing completion dates and the actual initial **2.22** process of ascertaining whether everyone in the chain is ready to exchange, it is in this area that the chain matrix should come into its own. Provided all the conveyancers involved in a chain "play the game" and feed the information about their client's progress into the matrix system, it should make the whole chain more transparent and should simplify arranging exchange and completion dates. There has to be a slight worry that, with the pressures of every day practice, some conveyancers may be less conscientious than others in completing the matrix. Regrettably, there will also be some who deliberately choose not to place accurate information on the matrix. But the conscientious conveyancer under the present system already has to cope with the less efficient, or the downright dishonest, and if the chain matrix can assist in this difficult task of synchronisation in any way at all, it will be welcomed.

Under the present paper-based system it is not usual to protect a **2.23** contract by entering a notice on the register—except in cases where completion has been set for a distant date, or in cases of options or pre-emptions. Because of this there is always a risk— albeit very slight—of a subsequent disposition being registered which would take priority over the buyer's contract. But the beauty of a totally electronic system is that such an entry will be made automatically, by the system itself, without any need for an express application to be made.

The transfer will then be drafted and approved in the usual way—but electronically. Similarly the mortgage deed will be drafted. Both documents will then be signed electronically. The Land Registry system will again check the content of the contract and mortgage to ensure that it complies with the details on the Register.

There is apparently no provision in the new system for the sub- **2.24** mission of "requisitions" between exchange and completion, as happens in the present system. Of course, years ago, title was only deduced after exchange, and requisitions were necessary to sort any apparent defects in the title. But today, title is always deduced prior to exchange and title defects dealt with at that stage. The requisitions form commonly used in residential transactions is now called the "Completion Information and Requisitions on Title Form". It deals with three separate matters. It starts by requesting confirmation that the answers supplied by the seller to the pre-contract enquiries remain the same and then moves on to the arrangements for completion—where will completion take place, etc. It also includes an undertaking by the seller's conveyancers to discharge the existing mortgage on the property. Will any of these be needed under the electronic system?

2.25   It must surely be relevant to know whether the answers to pre-contract enquiries remain the same. To be fair, a change would not necessarily justify the buyer in rescinding the contract—it would depend upon the enquiry in question and the terms of the contract—but sometimes it might. But there is nothing to prevent buyers sending an email to the sellers asking for confirmation of this.

As far as the arrangements for completion are concerned, this is no longer an issue. Completion will take place electronically and thus it can be effected in all transactions in the chain simultaneously. This will thus eliminate the other conveyancer's nightmare of not being able to send the money all the way along the chain on the same day. This can result in the last link in the chain completing on their sale—and so having to move out of their house—but being unable to complete on their purchase and having no new house to move into. This has resulted in at least one conveyancer having to house the client overnight in his own home!

Similarly, there will be no need for buyers to worry about the discharge of existing mortgages; these will again be effected automatically all along the chain on completion.

2.26   What about pre-completion searches? Under the present system a Land Registry search is required—and maybe other searches as well. What is the position under e-conveyancing? A pre-completion search at the Land Registry will not be required as there will no longer be a registration gap to worry about—see 2.27. But presumably the lenders will still require a bankruptcy search against the prospective borrowers and will still require that search certifying if entries are apparently received against the name of the prospective borrower. Similarly, a company search will also still be required against any seller that is a company, to reveal any floating charges and to ensure that the company still exists. Also, under para.5.11 of the Lenders' Handbook, a company search is required against any management company running a block of flats, and this too will still be required.

The transfer and mortgage will be signed ready for completion, as in the present system—but again these will be electronic documents signed with electronic signatures. Shortly before completion the parties to the transaction (and all parties in the chain) will signal their readiness to complete in accordance with the terms of the contract. They will do so by using an extension of the chain matrix, which will indicate first, that all necessary documentation is signed and, secondly, that all the financial arrangements are in place.

The conveyancers will thus still have to sort out the financial **2.27** arrangements as under the present system. Sellers must obtain redemption figures for any existing mortgages. Buyers conveyancers must prepare final statements for their client and ensure that they are in funds ready for completion from both buyer and lender clients ready for completion.

On completion the registers for all the transactions will be automatically changed. The seller's name and mortgage will be removed and the buyer and his mortgage inserted as per the notional register created from the contract stage. The registration gap—and the need for a pre-completion search to establish a priority period to protect against last minute entries—is thus avoided.

Under the present system, completion is far from the end of the **2.28** conveyancer's work. The seller must comply with his undertaking and discharge all existing mortgages, but as already seen, this will no longer be necessary. Equally the buyer has quite a large amount of work to do. The SDLT return must be completed and the tax paid. On receipt of the SDLT certificate application must then be made to the Land Registry to register the transaction, and the appropriate fee paid. But under the electronic system none of this will be required. Registration will have taken place simultaneously with completion. And as for SDLT, the return will still need making and the tax paying but this will now be done on-line. Indeed, many conveyancers are already doing this on-line now. But this will all be done on completion, not after it. To quote from the Land Registry web site:

> "All financial obligations, including Stamp Duty Land Tax and Land Registry fees as well as payments between buyers, sellers, lenders and conveyancers, will be settled through the EFT service. With the help of e-technologies, the amounts of Stamp Duty Land Tax and Land Registry fees will be correct in virtually all cases. This will contrast with the present high incidence of errors."

ELECTRONIC SIGNATURES

The system of e-conveyancing is going to be dependent on the **2.29** use of electronic signatures. The Electronic Communications Act 2000 gave power to the Government to change the formalities required for contracts and transfers of land. Documents signed using digital signatures would be deemed to comply with the requirements of the Law of Property (Miscellaneous Provisions) Act 1989 relating to contracts and deeds. At the moment a contract for the sale of land has to be in writing and signed by both parties. A deed must be signed, witnessed and delivered.

Obviously, an electronic contract or transfer could not comply with these requirements.

Digital signatures are not new—indeed we all make use of a simple form of one when we use our Personal Identification Number ("PIN") to obtain money from a cash machine or authorise payments to our credit cards. But there are worries about how secure these will be—see Chapter 5 "Will it Work?".

2.30   This is not the place, even if the author were capable of doing it, for explaining the technical details of how the proposed e-signatures would work, and this is the problem. The technology is so complex, that most of us have no idea how it will work or if it will work. You can see an ordinary hand written signature, but an electronic one is a string of codes in a computer file and most people have trouble enough understanding how computers work without trying to understand how an electronic signature works.

The favoured system seems to be Public Key/Private Key system. A digital signature is a computer file that accompanies the electronic document. It verifies that the document was signed by a particular person, and the content of the document hasn't been changed in any way, not even a single character, since it was signed. Everyone using the system will be issued with a private and a public "key". Keys are basically a string of computer codes. In order to make this work, the signatory of a document needs to obtain and install a special computer file called a certificate. Some trusted central authority will issue the certificate.

2.31   The Land Registry trialed a Digital Authentication Prototype recently and the user guide (obtainable on the Land Registry web site) sets out in detail the computer technology underlying the use of electronic signatures. Most of it is written in computer speak and so is difficult to understand, but it includes the following example of how the system works:

> "1. The sender (Alice) uses a one-way hash function to compute a small digest of her document. Using her private key, she encrypts the digest, turning it into a digital signature. The signature and the document may then be encrypted using the recipient's (Bob's) public key (for privacy) and transmitted.
>
> 2. Bob uses his private key to decrypt the document and derive the still-encrypted signature. Using Alice's public key, he decrypts the signature back into the sender's digest and then recomputes a new digest from the document. If the digests match, the document is authenticated"

2.32   The writer, at least, is not sure that he is any the wiser after this explanation! And in case you are not sure what a "hash" is, that is explained as follows:

"Hash

A fixed-size result obtained by applying a mathematical function (the hashing algorithm) to the data supplied (possibly a password or a longer message). Usually, a hash value will be much shorter than the original data. Most importantly, a hash is a one-way function. It is considered to be impossible (currently) to compute the original data (back) from the hash."

And in case we are not sure what an algorithm is:

"Algorithm

An algorithm is a mathematical function that is used to encrypt and decrypt information. There are many types of algorithm:

DES (Data Encryption Standard)—A symmetric key algorithm dating back to the late 70s. It is a block cipher with a 56 bit key. It is not seen as strong enough encryption for today's computers.
Tripe-DES—Makes DES more secure by using it 3 times with different keys (total key length of 168 bits).
RSA (Rivest, Shamir and Adelman)—A widely used Public Key Cryptography system. Can be used for encrypting information and as the basis for digital signatures.
SHA-1 (Secure Hash Algorithm–1)—Developed and published by the National Institute of Standards and Technology (NIST—a US agency) in 1994. The algorithm creates a 160 bit message digest from a message up to 2^{64} bit long."

In his Newsletter for August 2003, Bob Ballard of Textor.com **2.34** tried to explain the concept of electronic or digital signatures by use of an analogy. In case this is any clearer, this was as follows:

"This is complicated stuff, but I will try to explain this with a little story that hopefully will help explain the basic concepts. . .

Once upon a time. . .

There was a Chinese emperor who wanted to send valuable presents to his cousins who lived in far-off lands. However, he was worried that the merchants would substitute cheap copies en-route. He had his chief locksmith create a set of small boxes which had a very special type of lock. The lock needed two keys, one to lock it and a different key to unlock it (this may seem a bit strange but you have to admit the possibility).

The emperor had only one 'lock key', but had many copies of the 'unlock key' made and sent them to all his cousins. Now if he wanted to send a present—for example a vase, he had his artists make drawings of the vase and put them in the little box. Then he locked the box and sent it with the vase to his cousin.

When his cousin got the present, he unlocked the box and checked the vase against the drawing. Provided everything matched, he knew it hadn't been tampered with. The emperor must have sent it because only he could have locked the box in the first place. He knew the vase hadn't been replaced because he had checked the very detailed information in the box.

But. . .

But how did the cousin know that the unlock key he received in the first place was really from the emperor.

The answer is simple. The emperor used the same system to send out the unlock keys. However, this time the little box with the picture of the key in it came from the chief lock-smith. The chief locksmith's unlock keys were widely distributed and everyone had a copy somewhere in their house, so nobody could substitute a fake.

When the cousin received the key from the emperor he unlocked the little box using the chief's unlock key, checked the picture and put the emperors key on his keyring safe in the knowledge that it was genuine.

What have Chinese emperors got to do computers?

As implemented in the computer world this gets mind-bendingly complex. The equivalent of the picture and the box is a computer file called a *digital signature*. The equivalent of the chief locksmiths box and picture is called a *certificate*. The equivalent of the chief locksmith is a central certification authority such as Verisign, Inc.

However they can delegate to other authorities so you potentially get a chain of certificates—called a certification path. I didn't cover that in the story but you probably get the drift by now."

Well, yes, I hope that we all did get the drift! It is quite compli- **2.35** cated. But, as previously stated, that is the problem—it is quite complicated and could be beyond the understanding of many. Also, people do not like things that they do not understand. Most of us will be taking this all on trust.

ELECTRONIC FUNDS TRANSFER

One of the major problems with modern day conveyancing **2.36** practice is the need to complete all transactions in a chain on the same day. Clients are usually not able to move into rented accommodation for a day or two to allow the conveyancing to be completed. The particular problem on the day of completion is the need to move the money from one buyer to seller and so on all the way up the chain. Due to the constraints of the present banking system, even with computerised transfers, it is always difficult to ensure that this can be successfully achieved, particularly in a long chain of transactions. The Land Registry proposes to introduce a new form of Electronic Funds Transfer system which will enable near simultaneous transfers of money all along the chain, thus solving at least one of the conveyancer's nightmares.

In April 2005, the Land Registry published a consultation paper **2.37** on the new EFT scheme, which suggested the use of an "Agent Bank" system. Although 89 per cent of respondents to the consultation thought the system workable, some doubts were expressed about certain aspects of the scheme and further consultation is to be undertaken. The Land Registry will also appoint banking consultants to advise on banking systems and protocols. As a result the EFT system will not be used in the e-conveyancing pilot to be launched next year.

So what is an "Agent Bank" and how would the scheme work? The idea is that the Land Registry would appoint a bank (the Agent Bank) to operate the scheme for it. All the parties to a chain will pay all necessary funds required to complete the transaction—including Land Registry fees and SDLT as well as the purchase price—into the Agent Bank prior to the day fixed for completion. It is suggested that this should be done no later than midday on the day before completion. At the same time, the parties' conveyancers will also provide details of all the payments to be made on their particular transaction. The Agent Bank will then be able to confirm that all monies necessary to complete all transactions in the chain are in its hands. Assuming this to be the case, at the time fixed for completion, the Central Service will instruct the Agent Bank to make all the necessary payments. These can then be made within a very short timescale—say 30 minutes.

2.38   In case of last minute problems, there will also be the facility available for any conveyancer in the chain to revoke the execution of the transaction right up to the time fixed for completion. This would deal with a situation where a buyer found just before completion, e.g. that there was a sitting tenant occupying the premises.

The potential benefits of this system for all concerned in a conveyancing transaction are obvious—no worries about whether the money will arrive in time from the buyer to send it on to your seller. But the Land Registry acknowledges that there are problems. The Land Registry's consultation document points out that as funds will need obtaining a day earlier, there will be a loss of interest on such monies. Equally, as the mortgage funds will need obtaining a day earlier, this could result in extra interest being payable. The Land Registry estimates that on a loan of £100,000 at 5 per cent this would result in an extra payment of £13.70 per day. This would of course be more significant over a weekend.

2.39   Many practical conveyancers would immediately think of the difficulties that they have in getting cleared funds in time for the day of completion. Having to get them in for the day before would add to the pressure. It might be the case, therefore, that a longer gap between exchange and completion would have to be agreed in order to enable the funds to be obtained on time. It would indeed be ironic if the system of electronic conveyancing, designed to speed up transactions, did actually result in slowing them down!

But if it can be made to work, it will indeed be a great improvement over the present system. However, as one conveyancer commented after reading the Land Registry's proposals: "Well, if the banks can do everything this quickly, why aren't they doing it for us now?"

Chapter 3

Where are we now?

Initially, when e-conveyancing was first mooted, the Land **3.01**
Registry intended that it should be introduced with a big-bang
approach that would be piloted in 2005. However, after
consultation with "stakeholders", the Land Registry decided at an
early stage that it should be implemented on an incremental basis.
The pilot of the full service was then retargeted for 2006 and has
now slipped again to 2007 (see below). As the Land Registry web
site states:

> "We are very conscious of the common causes of failure
> experienced by some large business' change programmes in
> both the public and private sectors. One such cause is to
> introduce change as a "big bang". Our aim throughout the
> programme is to introduce new services incrementally, in
> steps that will be manageable for all users. Land Registry
> has already launched a number of electronic services in this
> way."

On the Land Registry Direct web site there is also the following
message from Peter Collis, Chief Land Registrar and Chief
Executive:

> "We strive to be recognised as the most professional,
> efficient and courteous public service in the United
> Kingdom. We will build upon our reputation as a highly
> successful executive agency to become a world-class
> provider of land registration services and information—an
> organisation which continuously strives to improve the
> quality of its service to customers; which brings together the
> best aspects of public service and which facilitates commerce
> by providing the confidence and security necessary for a
> stable market economy."

It is, therefore, clear that the Land Registry takes the view that the object in introducing e-conveyancing is to further that aim— not to prejudice it. The Land Registry is generally very well regarded by conveyancers—both in absolute terms and in its management of new projects (unlike, for example, HM Revenue and Customs in its introduction of SDLT), and so it will have the confidence of the profession in its implementation of e-conveyancing. However, the Land Registry has realised that it is important that it gets e-conveyancing right first time round or otherwise it might lose the support of the profession (and others) with regard to the whole concept.

CURRENTLY AVAILABLE ELEMENTS OF E-CONVEYANCING

3.02   So, in furtherance of this incremental basis, there are various parts of the e-conveyancing "package" that are already available for use by conveyancers. And just as the Land Registry are introducing e-conveyancing incrementally, so must the profession. There is an element in the legal profession that prefers to stick its head in the sand and ignore the future, hope it will go away, say that they will have retired before it comes in, and so they need not concern themselves with e-conveyancing. In Chapter 4 "Getting Ready for E-Conveyancing" it is strongly argued that those conveyancers not yet making use of the services that are currently available ought to start doing so immediately—otherwise when e-conveyancing becomes compulsory, they will have to bring it in as a "big-bang", with all the risks to the viability of the firm if it all goes wrong—to say little of the extra stress on staff having to cope with a completely new system all at once. Conveyancers must, therefore, adopt the Land Registry approach themselves—bringing the new procedures into use incrementally as and when they become available.

So what elements of the final e-conveyancing package are available now? Is your firm making full use of them? If not, why not?

LAND REGISTRY DIRECT

3.03   Direct access by conveyancers to the Register has been available for some years now and is now called Land Registry Direct. Initially this was introduced as a dial-up service, but since 2004 has been internet based. This has increased reliability and there has been a greatly increased take-up by conveyancers (and others such as mortgage lenders and estate agents) since that time. It seems strange that there are still conveyancers around who do not make use of it and continue to use the old fashioned paper-and post-based access to Land Registry services. With Land

Registry Direct, matters that used to require the filling in of a paper form and then sending it through the post and getting a reply back "in course of post", can be dealt with on your computer almost instantaneously. Why wait? If nothing else think of the postage you will save.

The following services are currently available electronically **3.04** using Land Registry Direct:

- The ability to view Registers, title plans and scanned documents.

- To request and obtain Official Copies (with or without the title number being known).

- To make and receive Index Map searches.

- To make and receive Land Registry searches of the whole of a title with priority.

- To make and receive Land Charges (including bankruptcy) searches.

As electronic conveyancing progresses, more and more services will become available by direct access. The Land Registry's e-lodgment scheme (see below) has now introduced the possibility of making applications to change the Register itself electronically.

Electronic lodgement (forms and deeds)

Since February 2002, conveyancers have been able to make **3.05** simple non-dispositionary applications electronically using Land Registry Direct. These included noting on the register a change of name and/or address of a registered proprietor. This was followed up in February 2005 with a pilot scheme for the electronic lodgement of applications that require Land Registry forms to be attached, such as entering a restriction on the register.

Again, like Electronic Discharges of Mortgages (see below), this is real electronic conveyancing, rather than just obtaining copies of documents and making searches electronically. And this is e-conveyancing that any practitioner subscribing to Land Registry Direct can make use of. It is not just limited to mortgage lenders as the e-discharge scheme is. So, as stated before, it is best to start making use of it whenever we can so we can start getting used to the new ways of doing things.

At the time of writing, the following types of application could **3.06** be made using e-lodgement:

- Application to be registered as a person to be notified of an application for adverse possession.

- Application to cancel a caution against dealings.

- Change of property description.

- Change of address.

- Change of name by marriage or deed poll.

- Death of a joint proprietor.

- Application for registration of a notice of home rights.

- Application for renewal of registration in respect of home rights .

- Application for cancellation of a home rights notice.

- Application to enter a standard form of restriction.

- Application for an order that a restriction be disapplied or modified.

- Application to withdraw a restriction.

- Application to enter a unilateral notice.

- Application to remove a unilateral notice.

- Application for the cancellation of a unilateral notice.

- Application for upgrading of a title.

- Application to withdraw a caution.

NATIONAL LAND INFORMATION SERVICE CHANNELS

3.07   The Land Registry was also instrumental in developing the National Land Information Service ("NLIS") service. It became operational early in 2001 and is intended as a one-stop shop for conveyancers (and others) enabling electronic access to a wide range of information, in particular offering the facility to make searches electronically. There is a central "hub" with access to the information being provided by three commercial "channels". The hub is managed by The Council for the National Land (and Property) Information Service, a not for profit Community Interest Company.

The three channels currently licensed are TM Search, MDA Transaction Online and Searchflow. NLIS is currently actively encouraging more commercial organisations to apply to become licensed channels. At the time of writing, the system has undertaken over seven million searches. The channels are also able to provide searches and other information from the Land Registry such as Official Copies and priority searches.

3.08   The channel thus allows all searches that a conveyancer might wish to make in a transaction to be requested electronically by ticking a few boxes. This saves the time and expense of making separate paper based searches. Many of the search results are then sent electronically, resulting in a much speedier and more efficient service all round. Ultimately, all search results will be provided electronically. One cloud on the horizon, however, is the tortuously slow progress of local authorities in electronically connecting to NLIS. Without this connection many local searches still come back through the post weeks after being requisitioned. It is sad that Government, so keen to implement HIPs could not have spent more resources on securing electronic connections between all local authorities and the NLIS hub. If the results of local searches could be received in a matter of minutes (as they already can be from many local authorities), many have argued that HIPs would no longer be required.

ELECTRONIC NOTIFICATION OF DISCHARGES

3.09 One of the features of the present paper based method of conveyancing that will disappear with e-conveyancing is the need after completion for the seller to arrange the discharge of any existing registered charges on the title and then arrange the removal from the Register of the entry protecting such charge. This was traditionally achieved by the lender executing an authority in Form DS1 to remove the charge from the register, which then had to be submitted by post to the Land Registry for the removal of the charge from the Register to be made manually by a Land Registry official.

3.10 However, over the last few years, the Electronic Notification of Discharge ("ENDS") has now become the routine way of notifying the Land Registry of the discharge of a legal charge. The seller's conveyancer sends the amount required to discharge the mortgages to the lender in the traditional way. However, the lender then notifies the Land Registry electronically of the discharge. This electronic notification dispenses with the need for the conveyancer to lodge a formal paper discharge obtained from the lender. It thus saves time (and expense) for lenders and for seller's conveyancers. However, it is not e-conveyancing. It is still necessary for a Land Registry official to action the END by actually removing the charge in question from the register. But it is a good example of the use of modern technology in the conveyancing process.

ELECTRONIC DISCHARGES

3.11 This is a major development that will ultimately replace ENDs entirely and is "real" electronic conveyancing in use now. Under the Electronic Discharge ("ED") scheme, following redemption of a legal charge affecting registered land, an electronic instruction is sent by the lender to the Land Registry, authorising cancellation of the relevant entries. The service operates totally in a computer to computer environment. The message is validated electronically and provided that this is in order, the legal charge entries are removed automatically from the register. There is thus no longer a need for a manual removal by a Land Registry official. The Land Registry normally receives the instruction within five working days of the redemption and the electronic process takes only a matter of seconds to complete. The scheme was piloted by Abbey and Nationwide and was very successful. It is expected that other major lenders will join the scheme shortly.

LAND REGISTER ON-LINE

3.12   In addition to Land Registry Direct, which is aimed at professional users, the Land Registry also offers a system which is aimed at the general public. It enables copies of the register and title plan to property to be viewed online and to be printed off in return for a small fee payable on-line by credit or debit card. Certain filed documents are also available for view and purchase. Although aimed at the general public, property professionals have been known to make use of the service as it is (alleged) to be quicker and easier to view a title using this system rather than using the NLIS channels or Land Registry Direct.

CHAIN MATRIX PILOT

3.13   In February 2006, the Land Registry announced a pilot of one of the key elements of e-conveyancing—and also one of its most controversial elements—the chain matrix scheme. This is to be piloted in Bristol, Fareham and Portsmouth, between Autumn 2006 and Spring 2007. Liz Hirst, director of the Land Registry's e-conveyancing programme, said:

> "We believe that around one quarter of residential chains fall apart at the moment, and our online chain matrix service aims to reduce this misery.
>
> The prototype will test how easy the chain matrix is to use and help us to assess what effect it will have for our customers. Volunteers participating in Bristol, Portsmouth and Fareham will be representative of future users, and we will listen very carefully to their feedback as we develop our services for the future."

Some might say that the choice of Bristol as one of the pilot areas is unfortunate following its use by the Government as the location of the notorious Home Information Pack pilot of a few years ago. This pilot was used to prove the case for HIPs, which very few conveyancers are in fact convinced of. Some have suggested that the Government went into the HIPs pilot with its mind already made up to bring in HIPs. One has to hope that the Land Registry has a more open mind as to the whole concept of a Chain Matrix, or again the results of the pilot could prove controversial.

The pilot will be voluntary, which is probably inevitable, but it **3.14** is hoped that a sufficient number of chains will take part so that proper experience of the chain matrix' utility can be gained. Many say that the small number of completed transactions involved was one of the problems in the Bristol HIPs pilot.

Fortunately, the Land Registry has a very good record of heeding consultation with the profession (e.g. the withdrawal of the proposals for prescribed form leases in 2003) and any concerns over the pilot will probably be groundless. Indeed, the good thing is that the Land Registry is conducting this as a pilot in the first place, rather than just going ahead anyway. Hopefully it will go well and there will be a worthwhile number of transactions involved so a realistic analysis can be made. If the chain matrix does help to stop residential chains "falling apart" then it will be welcomed by all concerned, but how it can stop a buyer or seller changing their mind about a property or make a mortgage lender speed up the offer of a loan, remains to be seen.

E-CONVEYANCING PILOT

It is nearly here! The Land Registry announced in April 2006 **3.15** that a pilot of the e-conveyancing system itself would be launched in October 2007. This, like the chain matrix, is again to be on a voluntary basis. It seems likely that more conveyancers will volunteer for this pilot than for the chain matrix pilot. Many will see it as a marketing tool—particularly volume conveyancers and those firms who already offer conveyancing services on-line. Many firms also already allow clients to track the progress of their transaction on-line. Indeed, one wonders why any firm would *not* want to be a part of this pilot. Otherwise, clients—and particularly the young who are so accustomed to using the computer in virtually every aspect of their lives—will vote with their feet and go to those firms who do offer the system, even though it may turn out in reality that their particular transaction cannot be carried out electronically.

The worry, of course, is the number of transactions that can be completed using e-conveyancing. Quite how it will be ensured that both the buyer's and seller's conveyancers in any one transaction are both part of the pilot remains to be seen. Presumably, it will not be possible to restrict a buyer's choice of conveyancer, so even though the seller's conveyancer may be e-conveyancing enabled, presumably if the buyer's is not, the transaction would then have to be conducted in the old fashioned way. And equally, if the buyer's conveyancer was electronically enabled and the seller's was not.

3.16   Equally, the bane of a residential conveyancer's life is the chain transaction and it is hoped that the operation of e-conveyancing in such a context can be piloted. But if it is going to be difficult to ensure that both sides in a simple stand alone transaction are both e-conveyancing compliant, it will be even harder to ensure that all of those involved in a chain will be able to conduct all of the links in a chain of transactions electronically.

We are told that the choice of date (October 2007) follows consultation with "stakeholders", who have indicated that the housing market's quieter period between October and January would be the best time to launch the new system. The date has also been chosen to give the industry time to adjust to HIPs, which will be introduced on June 1, 2007. It is to be hoped that conveyancers do not tar e-conveyancing with the same brush as HIPs and treat them both with similar contempt.

3.17   The Land Registry Chief Executive, Peter Collis was also reported as giving an indication as to when e-conveyancing would become compulsory for all transactions, saying

> "Stakeholder feedback has helped us to identify a preferred date for implementing compulsory use of the electronic system by 2009 or 2010. We will continue to listen to the stakeholder community and to refine our plans as appropriate."

Apparently, we are told, e-conveyancing "is a central pillar of the government's agenda to modernise public services".

One has to point out to conveyancers that 2010 might sound light years away, but it is in fact less than four years away. All the more reason to start preparing now. And yes, that date might slip—but then again it might not. But whether it slips or not, there can be no downside to getting ready now for e-conveyancing, whether it is implemented in 2010 or 2012.

3.18   The proposed Electronic Funds Transfer System that will eventually underpin the whole of e-conveyancing, is to be excluded from the pilot pending further consultation with stake-holders and the appointment of banking consultants to advise on banking systems and protocols. This must be sensible. The idea of all the payments in every link in the chain being made almost simultaneously sounds wonderful, but it has to be done correctly. Conveyancers already have enough problems with transferring money, without creating new ones. Presumably, therefore, the current methods of money transfer through the Clearing House Automated Payments System ("CHAPS") will be used. This will, of course, remove some of the benefits of e-conveyancing when it comes to the ease of completing a chain of transactions. However, it must be sensible, as the Land Registry have emphasised throughout, to adopt this step at a time approach, rather than trying to pilot everything at once. If the rest of e-conveyancing can be piloted now, then best to do so, rather than waiting for the EFT system to be available.

CONCLUSION

So the elements that together will make up e-conveyancing are **3.19** slowly but surely taking shape. If all conveyancers embrace the changes with an open mind it will be a success. But success depends on careful planning by all concerned, not just the Land Registry. You (or your business) cannot afford to wait. Start preparing now!

Chapter 4

Getting Ready For E-Conveyancing

Introduction

4.01   Whether we like it or not, e-conveyancing is coming so we must be ready for it. It is, perhaps, the biggest challenge the conveyancing profession has faced since the introduction of registered land itself. However, the profession has faced and survived many challenges in recent years—a new Land Registration Act, SDLT (well, OK, we just survived it!), changes to adverse possession, etc, and we can also survive the introduction of e-conveyancing. What makes it different to some of the other changes is, it might actually make things better both for our clients and for ourselves.

However, to achieve this we must be ready for it. As in all things, preparation is the key. We cannot stick our heads in the sand and hope that it will go away, nor can we simply say (as many seem to be doing) "It won't affect me as I am going to retire before it comes in". Some people are already making comparisons with the introduction of the 1925 property legislation when, allegedly, large numbers of property lawyers retired. Many are now saying they will do so to avoid e-conveyancing. Why? E-conveyancing has been deliberately designed to use well-established computer techniques. There is no reason why anyone accustomed to using a Windows based computer and accessing the internet, will not be able to undertake an electronic transaction. We have nothing to fear from it and everything to gain.

4.02   In any event it will ultimately (maybe from as early as 2009!) be compulsory to undertake conveyancing in this way, so if a firm is to remain in business long-term, we will have to adopt the system—and adapt to it, whether we like it or not. And of course, from a business point of view, it has to be the sooner the better. Those firms who are equipped to handle e-conveyancing will inevitably have a marketing tool which will give them the edge when it comes to attracting business. This could make itself felt as early as next year when the e-conveyancing pilot is introduced.

Doing things the old fashioned way may be attractive in certain circumstances but most members of the public these days seem to want quick, cheap, easily accessible services in every area in which they are involved—and the internet plays a large part in this in most people's eyes. There is every reason to suspect that they will favour similar services when it comes to buying and selling property and this is what e-conveyancing will be perceived to offer.

It is always said that the future belongs to the young, and there is no doubt that the young people of today are accustomed to using computers in almost every aspect of their lives—whether it is on a daily basis in their working environment, to using the internet to buy everything from groceries to holidays. People bank on the internet, book their holidays on the internet, use computers to play games and watch films. It is inevitable that they will take the buying and selling of houses electronically for granted. A good businessman or woman must always give the customer what they want if their business is to succeed.

When e-conveyancing comes, we must be ready, both as regards **4.03** the equipment in our offices and also our state of mind. There is no point fighting against the inevitable. To be harsh, it will probably be better for the success of the system (and individual firms) if those individuals who are unable to approach e-conveyancing at least with an open mind, *do* retire. But why not give it a try? What have you got to fear? We manage to survive the introduction of SDLT and the complexities of Form SDLT1 (and the others), so after that e-conveyancing will be a piece of cake!

What do we need to be able to undertake e-conveyancing? The Land Registry have published on their web site "Planning Book 1", aimed at helping users identify their current working environment, and any changes required to improve their readiness to take part in e-conveyancing. It identifies three areas that firms will need to consider to make sure that they are ready to go when the time comes. These are the IT system itself, Staff Skills, and Auditing and Control Systems. These will be looked at separately.

SYSTEM REQUIREMENTS

The Land Registry booklet identifies five possible stages that an **4.04** organisation's IT system may have reached:

- Level 1. You have PCs on desks which are not yet linked to each other.

- Level 2. The PCs on your desks are networked to each other.

- Level 3. Your business processes have been redesigned to benefit from networked PCs.

- Level 4. Your system plugs into a network external to your organization.

- Level 5. You have redesigned your business to reflect the interaction of networks.

The Land Registry states that you need to be at Level 4 in order to be able to carry out the e-conveyancing procedures. One might add that one still hears rumours that some firms have not yet even moved to Level 1! Only recently an experienced conveyancer was heard to boast that he did not have a computer on his desk and never intended to have one!

4.05   Even though all this is quite technical, it is clear that any firm which already has networked computers with internet access, will be able to undertake e-conveyancing. A very large number of firms are already at that stage. For most, there will thus be no need to buy new, expensive hardware before a firm is e-conveyancing compliant. Some new software will be required in order to comply with the requirements for electronic signatures, but the Land Registry is very keen to ensure that as little as possible completely new software and hardware will be required.

Obviously, it makes sense for those who have not already reached Level 4 to start planning immediately so that they will be able to achieve this level as soon as possible. The point is that setting up the systems necessary for e-conveyancing will also greatly enhance the efficiency of the firm in other areas as well. For the majority of firms which are already making use of Land Registry Direct and/or one of the NLIS search channels, they are already likely to be virtually ready for e-conveyancing, both as far as IT systems and also staff skill levels are concerned.

STAFF SKILLS

4.06   According to the Land Registry, the IT skills needed to enable staff to use the e-conveyancing system and related internal processes are likely to include:

- Using the internet.

- Creating and amending contracts and other documents.

- Sending and replying to emails.

- Manipulating Microsoft Windows based systems.

- Use of case management system/forms software (if any).

In everyday English, all we are really looking for initially are basic word-processing skills—plus the skill and legal knowledge necessary to "create" and amend contracts. The use of the word "create" here (rather than draft) does, of course, very much smack of the de-skilling of conveyancing, but this has been in full flow for a long time. It is likely that e-conveyancing will accelerate that process. There is also a need for the ability to send and receive emails and generally use any Windows based computer programmes.

This does mean that most "support" staff already employed **4.07** will have most of these skills—as will most fee-earners. Only a few of the latter will have to brush-up or learn basic computer skills before they will be e-conveyancing ready. Firms that already require support staff to have basic computer skills, will already have in place procedures to induct new employees into the firm's own systems, so only slight additions will be required to provide an induction to those special matters unique to e-conveyancing.

AUDITING AND CONTROL SYSTEMS

The Land Registry advises that: **4.08**

"Your internal policies should aim to cover:

– disposal of e-requisitions
– general email policy
– general email maintenance, monitoring and controls
– internal electronic approval/authorization arrangements
– filing and processing incoming emails
– archiving of mixed paper/electronic case records."

Again, perhaps not written in the plain English that the Land Registry is usually so good at, but it can be readily discerned what is required here. Remember, we are talking about "policies" and "procedures", meaning that you must have systems (i.e. rules) in place as to who, how, and when all these various steps are taken. Most firms that already have internet access will already have such policies in place, e.g. as to how often email in boxes must be accessed and leaving electronic messages when a recipient of an email is out of the office, etc. These will obviously need reviewing to see how they are affected by the requirements of e-conveyancing, but then all good systems will include a processes for periodic review anyway.

There are other areas, in addition to those identified by the **4.09** Land Registry, which will need consideration.

Making use of the currently available elements of e-conveyancing

4.10   Already some of the parts of e-conveyancing are in place—and what better way of getting ready for e-conveyancing than making use of them?

We should be signed up to use Land Registry Direct and the NLIS channels. There is already no need to make searches or request Official Copies using paper forms and the ordinary post. Already all this can be done at the click of a mouse button. The Land Registry are deliberately introducing e-conveyancing in a phased manner, rather than in a big-bang, to ensure that each segment works. We need to take advantage of this and make use of each new procedure, each step forward, as soon as it is available. Otherwise, when e-conveyancing does become compulsory, it will all be new to us. We will have to get used to the whole new system overnight. And the danger is that we will be left behind struggling in the gutter whilst the well prepared storm ahead and steal all our business.

4.11   Look again at Land Registry Direct and the NLIS channels. Yes, there is a fee to use the NLIS channels over and above the cost of the searches themselves, but that is not the whole story. Even ignoring the saving of time in receiving the results of searches, many firms have found that the ease of making searches using NLIS and the savings in postage, staff time in completing separate application forms for each search required for a property, and bank charges on the separate cheques that would otherwise be needed, more than make up for this.

Just think of a property where it is necessary to make a local search and enquiries, a drainage and water search, a chancel repairs screening search, a coal mining search, a commons registration search, and an environmental search. Someone in the office has to type out all the request forms and put them into envelopes and submit them to the correct address. With NLIS it is only necessary to input the property details once and then click a few boxes with the mouse to indicate which searches are to be made. And in any event many conveyancers charge the NLIS fee as a separate disbursement. There is also the fact that some search applications are rejected and have to be resent due to errors in the application form. The NLIS channels validate the information about the target property before the search is submitted.

4.12   In deciding whether to switch to NLIS, conveyancers should also consider how they decide which searches might be relevant in an area. How do you know which searches might be relevant in an area hundreds of miles away? There are dozens of possible searches that can be made. Do you know them all? An NLIS channel will help you decide which ones are relevant to the property you are buying.

Think also of the time and money to be saved by being able to obtain Official Copies from the Land Registry on-line, or being able to obtain the result of an Official Search on-line. These benefits can be obtained now, and will stand the firm and its staff in good stead ready for e-conveyancing.

IT support

One area which will need careful consideration when we do **4.13** have e-conveyancing, is the level of IT support that your firm will have available. Bigger firms will have IT managers and specialists employed as part of their permanent staff. These in-house IT staff will be available, maybe 24 hours a day, to resolve any problems with systems and hardware or software. But many smaller firms rely on outside consultants to handle their IT problems—often as part of a follow up package agreed when the IT system itself was installed. These outside consultants will often guarantee to solve any problems within 24 hours of being notified. Already some firms have experienced the limitations of such arrangements. But think about what will happen with e-conveyancing if there are system problems in your office first thing on a Friday morning— the busiest day of the week for completions, and likely to remain so. At the moment, under the present paper-based system, it would be bad enough, but with e-conveyancing just how would you be able to complete any transactions without access to the Land Registry computer network on which the whole system is to be based? Having the matter resolved within 24 hours may well not be good enough. It is not clear at the moment what contingency plans (if any) are intended to deal with such situa-tions. It is, therefore, essential that consideration be given to ensuring that any internal computer problems can be resolved within as short a time scale as possible. It is a simple matter of survival—those firms which get themselves a reputation of having computer problems, will lose business. Also, it seems likely that access to the Land Registry network will be conditional on having proper IT support systems in place, and if a firm's Network Access Agreement was not renewed, that would mean that the firm would not be able to undertake conveyancing work at all.

Training

All firms should already have proper systems in place for staff **4.14** training and education—if only to ensure that fee earners comply with Law Society Continuing Professional Development ("CPD") requirements. Consideration should be given now as to what training will be necessary in e-conveyancing techniques for staff of all grades. Many staff will feel more confident in their anticipation of e-conveyancing if they can be sure that they will receive adequate training before its implementation. As with all changes to long established practice, staff attitudes will go a long way to deciding whether something is a success or a failure. Fee earners must be brought on board for e-conveyancing, so they look forward to it as an improvement and without any fear as to their ability to deal with it.

Training need not be expensive, either in monetary terms, or in terms of lost chargeable time. The Land Registry is keen to assist as much as they can and the Land Registry web site already carries several useful training modules. For example, there is an interactive e-conveyancing demonstrator as well as an e-lodgment training module. Both ought to be required viewing for all involved in the conveyancing process.

Conclusion

4.15   The message is clear. Make sure you are making full use of those aspects of the system presently available. Make sure that you have training systems in place to ensure that all staff—whether partners, other fee earners or support staff—can now make use of all aspects that are presently in place and are familiar with all of the Land Registry's proposals for the future. Familiarity, they say breeds contempt, but it also breeds confidence; confidence that when the system does come into force, staff will be able to use it without fear or earth-shattering change to their present procedures.

Chapter 5

Will It Work?

Introduction

Having seen why we are to get e-conveyancing and how it will **5.01** work, we come to the crucial question—will it work? In his August 2003 newsletter, Bob Browning, Managing Director of Textor.com, an internet technology company, predicted that e-conveyancing "will not fly". He went on to say:

> "The system will fall like a house of cards the first time a large transaction goes pear-shaped and gets reported on the nine o'clock news or the Daily Mail."

By November 2004, his view had changed slightly. "I change my prediction", he said, "it will crash and burn".

By August 2005, when the Government had let the contract to **5.02** IBM to prepare the IT for e-conveyancing, his views had not changed:

> **"£21 Million down the tubes—and that is just for starters**
>
> The government has let the first contact in its doomed e-conveyancing initiative. A snip at £21 m but I suspect this is the tip of the iceberg—or to use a more accurate analogy, the bow of the Titanic.
>
> I have covered in previous newsletters the subject of e-conveyancing and why it is set to crash and burn. Unfortunately the ill-judged attempt to replace paper contracts with digitally-signed electronic records may bring down other parts of the project which are sensibly aimed at modernising the whole conveyancing process."

In December 2005, he again returned to the topic:

"someone just pointed out that many estate agents are trying to develop conveyancing as a business. Would you let an estate agent who can barely measure up your kitchen, sign documents on a transaction worth (in Chiswick) around a million, on your behalf? The mind boggles."

5.03   I think that all of us involved in any way with the conveyancing process must hope that he is wrong. Unfortunately everyone has a "folk memory" of some vast computer project (usually a Government one) that has gone wrong at enormous expense. One can immediately think of criminal records, passports, National Health Service and the Child Support Agency. The Land Registry are, of course, keen to stress that they do not intend to go the same way—hence the incremental approach, rather than the big-bang. I am sure that none of those involved in past computer disasters actually went into them wanting, or intending, a disaster.

We are, however, very fortunate that the Land Registry is keen to pilot the system first before introducing it nationwide. Hopefully the pilots of the chain matrix and e-conveyancing itself—but without the key EFT system—will highlight any potential problems and so ensure a successful project. That, after all, is the object of having a pilot, but it will only be when the EFT system is bolted on that we will know for sure. The proof of the pudding will, therefore be in the eating—or in the pilot—but in the meantime we can, perhaps, make a few comments on the various aspects of the system and try to come to some conclusions.

COMPUTER PROBLEMS

5.04   "Computers can't be relied on. What if the system crashes?" This is the question that is always asked when conveyancing practitioners discuss e-conveyancing. But nothing that is being proposed is rocket science. The systems that will be used are, from a computing point of view, fairly straightforward in their application and design. Computers already control trains and aeroplanes, to say little of missile systems, so there is no reason at all why they should not be used to buy and sell land.

It is a very sad reflection on the computer industry as a whole that at a time when computers have been around for many years and are accepted as an essential tool in every business, that they are still regarded as being unreliable. It is perhaps fair to say that, as with many things, reports of computer problems are exaggerated, but everyone has stories of their own PCs crashing and losing lots of work or the problems in the office when the system is not available. No system is 100 per cent reliable and conveyancing at the moment can be delayed by problems with the post or telephone systems.

The Land Registry is well aware that the system has to work **5.05** right from the start and that any initial failures might result in the whole idea of electronic conveyancing being put on hold for many years.

> "We are very conscious of the common causes of failure experienced by some large business' change programmes in both the public and private sectors. One such cause is to introduce change as a 'big bang'. Our aim throughout the programme is to introduce new services incrementally, in steps that will be manageable for all users." (Land Registry Web Site—"The Story so Far")

This is obviously a very sensible approach and has been very successful in the systems rolled out so far. However, the problem with e-conveyancing is that it will rely on so many different systems for it to work effectively and most of them will not be under the Land Registry's control. The Land Registry's systems might work perfectly at all times, but it is not just the Land Registry's systems that need to work for e-conveyancing to be successful. To take a simple "chain" transaction:

X, a first time buyer is buying from Mr and Mrs Z. Mr and **5.06** Mrs Z are buying from Ms W who is in turn buying from A and B who are going into rented accommodation. There will be four firms of conveyancers involved, each with their own computer systems. A fault in any one of those systems at any time will delay matters; a fault on the day of completion will perhaps mean that none of these transactions can complete. How long would/ might it take for the solicitors acting for Mr and Mrs Z to rectify a fault in their system? A fault that might mean that they cannot access the internet or might prevent them accessing the relevant programmes or files on their server. Either way completion would not be possible. Many larger firms of conveyancers will have their own in-house IT specialists who can be relied on to resolve any problems quickly and effectively. But some smaller firms might rely on external consultants who only guarantee to solve problems within 24 hours. Hardly good enough.

There are also other possible problem areas. The whole system **5.07** is reliant on the internet and the numerous different internet service providers ("ISPs") used by each of the firms. ISPs sometimes have "downtime" due to internal problems. It would only need one ISP to have downtime on a Friday—the busiest day for completions—and the whole chain will be prevented from completing. The internet is generally reliant on the telephone system. This also is not immune from disruption. My own organisation recently had an external telephone problem—nothing to do with the organisation at all but at the phone company's premises—which took nearly 24 hours to resolve. So no internet, nor any phones either.

One can also foresee interesting questions arising when firm A's computer system crashes on a Friday and delays half a dozen transactions, as to who will foot the bill for wasted removal costs up and down the chain—will it be the client whose firm has the problem, or will the client rather expect the conveyancers to foot the bill? Or will conveyancing practice change? Will clients be allowed to move anyway and only the legal completion be delayed? After all, the legal work will have been completed and checked in advance and the money already transferred to the agent bank running the Electronic Funds Transfer system.

5.08   This would seem an attractive solution—at least at first sight. Maybe the Standard Conditions could be amended to make a contractual provision to this effect. Until then firms involved in electronic conveyancing will need to think very carefully about the liability they might be under if a lengthy chain is delayed due to a computer fault in their offices. Perhaps Special Conditions should be included in the contract to deal with this possibility. These could, perhaps, allow the buyer to take possession under a licence if completion cannot be effected due to IT problems. What about a provision providing that no interest was payable for the period of the delay? Everyone up and down the chain could then move and completion itself could then take place the next day—or whenever the technology was back in business. But like all good ideas, there has to be a downside. It is all well and good providing that no interest should be paid, but any delay will inevitably mean that any existing mortgages throughout the chain will be paid off at least one day later—and so one day's extra interest will have to be paid. Why should an innocent seller who was able and willing to complete have to pay this extra interest? No, the conveyancer whose IT system fails will have to pick up the bill all along the chain. But making provision for the clients to move in any event will at least mitigate that bill.

Just to emphasise that nothing can be straightforward, what about the participant in the chain who decides, at the last minute, that they do not want to proceed anymore? Maybe some last minute problem arises. As completion has not actually taken place, presumably they would still be able to withdraw, causing chaos everywhere if everyone has already moved. The only solution would be a contractual provision that no-one could refuse to proceed once the day fixed for completion had passed—after all the money would already have been paid into the agent bank ready for transmission by the EFT system. Is that an acceptable condition? One would need to think very carefully about agreeing to such a restrictive term.

Whilst we are thinking about the potential liability of conveyan- **5.09**
cers due to computer problems, imagine you are acting for the
buyer in a multi-million pound commercial transaction, where
time is of the essence as to completion. If completion was not
possible on the day fixed due to an IT problem, presumably the
"innocent" seller could, if he wanted to, immediately withdraw
from the contract and forfeit the buyer's deposit. That would
make a sizeable claim for the buyer to bring against his conveyancers. Maybe a provision in the retainer that the conveyancer will
not be liable for any loss caused by IT problems might be
attractive.

Conveyancers cannot behave like an ostriches and stick their
heads in the sand. We cannot go on thinking that conveyancing
cannot be dragged into the Twentieth Century (let alone the
Twenty First!). Computers cannot be uninvented. Systems have
got to change to meet client's expectations and we have to change
with them. We do need backup systems to deal with the
circumstances when there is a computer/internet problem as such
problems *will* occur—when rather than if. Hopefully not as regular
occurrences as some would have us believe, but it will be
inevitable. No-one so far seems to have come up with any sensible
contingency plans. On the FAQ section of the Land Registry's e-
conveyancing web site it is helpfully stated that "practitioners
may need to ensure that certain back up services are available to
enable them, for example, to operate from alternative premises
using somebody else's machinery". Quite how this would work
when all the information you require is on your own server which
you cannot access, is another matter.

Security issues: Computer systems

One of the many fears expressed about e-conveyancing is the **5.10**
question of security. If some teenager can hack into the
Pentagon's computer system, goes the story, then what chance is
there of making e-conveyancing safe? There will be widespread
fraud with people selling properties that don't belong to them and
diverting vast sums of money for their own purposes.

Certainly, the risks of fraud cannot be ignored, and the banks'
computer systems have not been immune to this. On November
26, 2004 the *Financial Times* reported a "rising tide of computer
fraud". Perhaps more worrying is the fact that it was also reported
that Detective Chief Superintendent, Ken Farrow, head of the City
of London Police Anti-fraud department said that "he was so
alarmed by the expertise used [by computer criminals] that when
he sold a house this year he went to a cash machine every day to
check the money in his account had not been stolen".

Even more worrying was the report on March 17, 2005 by **5.11**
Computer Weekly that police had foiled one of the world's biggest

attempted computer thefts when they prevented criminals stealing $400 million from the London branch of Japanese Bank Sumitomo Mitsui, after hacking into the bank's network. It was reported that "hackers managed to install remote key logging equipment on some of the bank's PCs to allow them to farm account numbers, passwords and other sensitive information . . .". With regard to the same incident, the BBC web site reported:

> "Richard Starnes, president of the Information Security Services Association, said: 'We have been talking about the doomsday scenario for quite some time and while this was not actualised it shows the magnitude of the threat to companies.'
>
> He told the BBC News Website: 'This will be discussed by chief executives and others for some time to come and it will further reinforce the need for corporate asset protection systems.'
>
> Mr Starnes, who works for Cable & Wireless, said key logging software—which detects every key stroke made by a keyboard and can give away crucial information such as passwords—was easy to obtain and quite simple to insert into a company's computers."

5.12   The worrying thing about e-conveyancing is that it depends upon so many different firms' computer systems. If someone could hack into the Land Registry system and simply change the names of registered proprietors on a few (multi-million pound) properties, they would then be able to easily sell those properties. They would after all look as though they were the real registered proprietors.

But that is not the real risk. Many thousands of conveyancing firms will be able to offer e-conveyancing. If key logging software really is so easy to obtain and install, then it would presumably be simple for someone to install it on a conveyancer's system and thus find details of passwords and key numbers and electronic signatures to enable them to fraudulently sell property by pretending to be that conveyancer. They would then also be able to direct the EFT to send the proceeds of sale to any nominated bank account they desired and then such account could be pre-programmed to send the money on to another account and so on until it became difficult to trace the ultimate destination. The interesting question here, of course, is that presumably the conveyancer in question whose system was attacked and misused in this way, would be personally liable for any loss suffered. After all, they will be responsible for the security of their own system. And to take an analogy, if some one hacked into your bank's computer system and then transferred money out of your bank account, you would expect the bank to make good the loss, wouldn't you?

One other problem with unauthorised sales of property is a little **5.13** less obvious. Assuming that you own a property that is "sold" without your authority, knowledge or consent, how do you prove that? If you have a digital signature, how do you prove that it was used without your authority? Because if you cannot prove the fraud, then you are not going to be able to get your property back or claim compensation for your loss. For both clients and conveyancers, the keeping of proper records showing that authorisation has been given by a client for the use of the conveyancer's digital signature, thus becomes of utmost importance. The security of digital signature will be looked at below.

There is also, of course, the possibility that someone could hack into the agent bank's system handling the EFT system and just divert funds to a fraudster's bank account.

Of course, everything is possible. Computer hackers could have **5.14** broken into the Pentagon computer system and launched hundreds of nuclear weapons, but they haven't. And if fraudsters want to hack into a bank's systems, why bother with the EFT system; just go for a major clearing bank. Why bother with the risk of selling properties for a few million pounds when a big hit at a clearing bank could steal hundreds of billions of pounds. And if hacking into banking systems were so easy and so common, then the whole worldwide banking system would have ground to a halt long before now. This is not to minimise the risk. Fraudulent use of the e-conveyancing system will happen sometime. What all concerned must do is to take all steps to reduce that risk as far as is possible. It is clear that one result of e-conveyancing might be to create lots of business for internet security firms!

The Land Registry web site contains the following "reassur- **5.15** ance" about security:

> "There are two questions here. The first is about network security and the second concerns the prevention of fraudulent dealings over the network. No system can be said to be totally secure. As soon as new security measures are introduced into computer systems then new ways of beating the system are found. All we can say at this stage is that we aim to incorporate the latest security systems into the build of the network and to review constantly the ability of these systems to defeat attempts to enter the system by unauthorised persons. For this reason it is unlikely that we will use the internet. It is more likely that we shall opt to use a private dedicated system.

On the question of fraud countermeasures, again, we intend to use the most modern and effective security systems available. We will, of course, have to rely on those practitioners who have been authorised to access the network to ensure that they take adequate steps to avoid breaches of security. It will be a strict condition in any network access agreement that practitioners must ensure that they keep their access codes and passwords totally confidential, and practitioners will, as now, have to take reasonable steps to ensure that the instructing client is indeed who he says he is.

Furthermore, we will certainly put in place audit trailing software that will identify when a particular practitioner used the network and precisely (possibly down to individual key strokes) what was entered on the system.

Two other points need to be remembered. The first is that any electronic system we devise must be at least as secure, and hopefully more secure than the current paper system, which in our experience can be subject to all kinds of fraudulent activity. When, after the event, we do discover that there has been a paper fraud it is extremely difficult to find out who perpetrated it. Secondly, we must emphasise that the Land Registry's indemnity fund will remain in place to compensate those who suffer loss as a result of fraud or error and we do not intend to place additional burdens on practitioners."

The suggestion that the internet itself might not be used is certainly reassuring; the warnings that reliance has to be placed on individual practitioners less so.

SECURITY ISSUES: DIGITAL SIGNATURES

5.16   The replacement of traditional written signatures by digital electronic signatures has been the subject of much thought and worry over security. In a way, this is rather strange. After all we have all been using various forms of digital signatures for years. Fifty years ago if one wanted to withdraw money from one's bank account, you had to write and sign a check and hand it over the counter to a cashier. You would then be signing to authorise the bank to pay you the money. But for many years now we have "signed" to authorise the bank to pay us the money by inserting a plastic card into a machine and typing in a Personal Identification Number ("PIN"). This is a very simple example of a digital signature. Yes, there is, allegedly, widespread fraud in the use of cash machines, but the speed and convenience of the system means that most us continue to use it anyway.

Similarly with credit cards we authorise a charge to our account now not by a signature but again by typing a PIN into a machine. As we all know, until February this year, it was usual when using a credit card to authorise a charge to the account by a hand written signature. But it was changed to the use of a PIN number in order to reduce the amount of fraud in a system based on signatures—signatures that could so easily be forged.

Much of this hysteria over the use of digital signatures is not **5.17** only unfounded but also hypercritical, as we already use them ourselves on virtually a daily basis. It could be argued that drawing money out of a bank account is slightly different than selling one's greatest asset. Yes it is, which is why the digital signatures envisaged will be somewhat more secure than a simple four digit PIN used for credit cards. Even Bob Ballard, whose forecast that e-conveyancing would "crash and burn" has been noted above says that: "If properly used a digital signature is much safer and fraud-proof than a regular signature." His fear is that it will not be properly used.

It is generally accepted that most clients will not have their own digital signatures and that the conveyancer would sign on their behalf. Indeed as Bob Ballard points out:

"If the house purchaser and seller is supposed to be doing this at home, they will need to:

- Install some MI6-grade software on their computer.
- Obtain a certificate.
- Install the certificate.
- Run the software to sign the document.
- Get the document plus signature to the solicitor for processing.

Someone somewhere might come up with some fancy way of packaging this up for the average punter who can't work their video recorder. But I remain unconvinced."

Is it the situation that the conveyancing documents would be **5.18** signed electronically by the conveyancer that causes Bob Ballard to claim that the system will "crash and burn". To quote from his November 2004 Newsletter:

"Instead of signing the various documents involved in house purchase, you will instead give authority to your conveyancer to sign them (digitally) on your behalf. So:

1. The conveyancer is changed from an administrator who shuffles paper around to a direct participant in a 6–7 figure transaction. This is not going to come without a price tag.
2. The signature on the documents doesn't go away, it is going to be held in an authorisation document held by your conveyancer (tick whichever applicable)
   - who just went out of business,
   - whose premises just burned down,
   - who had their files stolen
   - who just had a disgruntled employee walk out with their passwords and they haven't got round to changing them yet
   - who employed a clerk who transferred the whole portfolio of property to a relative in Hong Kong
3. Does anyone seriously think I am going to give anyone power of attorney to sign on my behalf for a transaction of this importance? No way baby.
   So this procedure is going to be
   - more expensive
   - riskier and
   - hard for customers to accept."

Now, of course, this is the view of someone who is a computer expert. Will a lay client really have such distrust in his conveyancer? One would hope not. So this must be an unduly pessimistic view of how clients will react to the new system. But it is a worry and certainly one well publicised fraud would result in a complete loss of confidence in the new system.

5.19   But Bob Ballard is not alone in his views. In December 2001. the Lord Chancellor's Department published the result of consultation on the e-conveyancing proposals. One of the questions asked of consultees was: "Do you agree that electronic signatures will be a satisfactory means of ensuring trust in electronic conveyancing documents?" Only 28 per cent of those answering the question agreed unconditionally that electronic signatures would be a satisfactory means of ensuring trust. Then 26 per cent thought that electronic signatures would definitely not be a satisfactory means of ensuring trust. Of the remainder, 44 per cent agreed with the statement subject to conditions, the most common being the implementation of a secure system—which rather seems to beg the question.

The Land Registry has recently piloted a Document Authentication Prototype for users of Land Registry Direct to "research and develop a solution for electronic signing in the e-conveyancing environment". This Prototype enabled users of Land Registry Direct to digitally sign applications for official copies (title known) and any e-lodged application forms. Three different methods of "signing" were used: These were:

- smart card

- USB token

- authentication grid

An evaluation report on this Prototype can be obtained on the Land Registry web site. The fact that these systems work does not address the issue as to whether it will be secure when it comes to actually transferring the ownership of property.

SECURITY: CONCLUSION

The real question we should be asking about fraud is whether **5.20** there will be more or less fraud under e-conveyancing than there is now under the present paper-based system. Fraud, particularly mortgage fraud, is widespread under the present system. Regrettably, this often involves conveyancing firms. One has to say that the Land Registry's decision to abolish the use of Land and Charge Certificates must have made conveyancing fraud easier than it was previously. But mortgage lenders were more than happy to "dematerialize". No doubt they calculated that the saving in storage costs would more than cover the increased losses possible because of this.

Only time will tell which system is the most secure. Forgery of **5.21** signatures—or indeed of entire conveyances—happens at the moment. The only protection against this is conveyancers carefully checking identification documents, to ensure that a seller/buyer/ borrower is who he says he is to ensure that some stranger does not impersonate, for example, a seller and sell that seller's property. Conveyancers already need to be very vigilant over ID checks, but, some are more vigilant than others. Some take the view that identity cannot be properly checked unless the client attends in person either at the conveyancer's offices or before some trusted intermediary. Some conveyancers simply require a client to confirm identity by sending their passport through the post and so never see that client. Anybody could have got hold of that passport and be sending it through the post.

The worrying thing about e-conveyancing is that all these present day possibilities for impersonation and forgery will still persist under e-conveyancing, but in addition we will have the risks caused by unknown persons hacking into conveyancers' or banks' or the Land Registry's computer systems to commit fraud, or by simply obtaining details of a conveyancer's electronic signature. It will be inevitable that some conveyancers will be less security conscious than others and Bob Ballard's fears about disgruntled employees making use of digital signatures must be a genuine cause for concern. It is hard to see how fraud can actually be reduced when e-conveyancing comes into compulsory use.

Consumer issues

5.22   There is another, more important aspect of the "Will it work?" question. The reason for introducing e-conveyancing is clear:

> "Our mission is to 'make conveyancing easier for all'—specifically, to develop an electronic system of conveyancing that makes buying and selling houses easier for the general public, conveyancing professionals, and other parties involved in the process." (the Land Registry web site—"The Story So Far")

This is what we should be asking when we wonder whether it will work. Will it make conveyancing easier for conveyancers and, most important of all, for our clients?

We all know that the present system is not perfect. It is cheap for consumers—compare the charges of estate agents—but it is slow and cumbersome. Will the new system make it quicker, and eliminate the present problems and bottlenecks? Are the current problems solely due to the present paper-based system or are there other reasons for delay?

5.23   As in all things, the Government seems to think that e-conveyancing will reduce conveyancing costs. Most conveyancers would say that costs are already cut to the bone and cannot be reduced any further. E-conveyancing will not reduce the amount of work that will need doing. Contracts and transfers will still need drafting and approving, search results will still need to be studied, indemnity insurance policies still argued over, enormous amounts of information given to HM Revenue and Customs, etc. As the same searches will still need making, the cost of disbursements will remain the same. (The introduction of HIPs might switch the cost of some of these to the seller, but they will still need doing and paying for by someone. Indeed, in the case of an HIP more than a few months old, they will need repeating by a buyer who will not be safe relying on an out-of-date search. The need for an Energy Performance Certificate in the HIP will inevitably increase the overall cost of moving home.) The only cost savings seem to be with regard to postage.

5.24   One cost that will *increase* is the cost of transferring funds. At the moment the banks charge a fee for money being transmitted through the CHAPS system to the seller. But under the e-conveyancing system there will be at least two transmissions; one from the conveyancer's bank account to the agent bank running the EFT to put the EFT in funds ready for completion, and then another series of transmissions from the EFT to the sellers, HM Revenue and Customs, the Land Registry, etc. As the agent bank will be a commercial operation, these will all need paying for and as the investment in setting up the agent bank and associated computer system is not going to be cheap, it could well be quite expensive.

It is difficult to see how the combined effect of HIPs and e-conveyancing will result in either the overall cost of moving home or conveyancers' charges themselves coming down, but that will probably not prevent Government claiming that they will/ should.

What about savings in time? Will it result in clients being able **5.25** to buy and sell and move home more speedily? Certainly, at the moment various documents are sent from one conveyancer to another through the post and the almost instantaneous transmission of documents by electronic means will save some time. But these days most conveyancers make use of fax (or even email) for contacting clients and the other professionals involved in the transaction already. Clients who do not themselves have (or wish for) contact by email) will still need to be contacted by post. Certainly conveyancers (and others) ought to be making more extensive use of these quicker methods of communication at the moment, so there must be some savings in time possible here but not very much.

As far as other aspects of the legal process are concerned, official copies and searches can already be made and results received electronically, as can searches through the NLIS channels. Not all firms make use of these facilities and a chain must proceed at the pace of the slowest link, so making e-conveyancing compulsory will speed up some chains, but that could be achieved more simply by making use of Land Registry Direct and the NLIS channels compulsory, without the need for full blown e-conveyancing.

The main delays in a conveyancing transaction can be listed as **5.26** follows:

- Obtaining mortgage finance.

- Receiving results of local searches.

- Conveyancing problems—discussing the need for indemnity insurance/obtaining instructions from buyer or lender clients, etc.

- Liaising to arrange completion dates along a chain.

- Someone in the chain not having found a buyer/property to buy.

- Delays in getting the funds in so as to be ready for completion.

No doubt many conveyancers can think of other causes of delays—delays by clients in supplying identification evidence, or delays by certain conveyancers, immediately spring to mind—but will e-conveyancing remove or reduce any of these delays?

MORTGAGE FINANCE

5.27   It is difficult to see how delays in obtaining mortgage finance will be eliminated. Lenders are very keen to emphasise that they are speeding up their systems but the need to check income, employment details, etc, has always to be carried out with care. Time could perhaps be saved over the undertaking of valuations and many lenders are now routinely making use of "desk top valuations" in the case of standard properties. Also, other aspects of lender's procedures could no doubt be speeded up—the length of notice needed for the mortgage advance to be sent to the conveyancer's bank account, or for the provision of a redemption figure, for example, but e-conveyancing is completely irrelevant to all this mortgage side of things. Time could be saved here whether or not we have e-conveyancing. Ironically, e-conveyancing could actually result in further delays. Under the EFT scheme as presently envisaged, all funds necessary for every transaction in the chain will have to be paid into the "agent bank" running the scheme at the latest by the day before completion. At the moment, as long as the money was in the conveyancer's account the actual day of completion, the transaction could still go ahead. It will not be able to under the new system. Presumably, details as to the payments out (e.g. mortgage redemption) will also need to be provided the day before—another possible cause of problems.

LOCAL SEARCHES AND ENQUIRIES

5.28   The other major cause of delays is obtaining the result of local searches. Will e-conveyancing help here? Well yes and no. The NLIS system can be seen as an integral part of e-conveyancing or as a stand-alone facility. Either way it is already in use by thousands of conveyancers —over seven million searches had been made through the three NLIS channels at the time of writing. So saving time during searches is already possible and will increase as more local authorities become fully involved in the system.

Assuming that by the time we have a fully working system of e-conveyancing, we also have HIPs in place, in many cases there will be no need for a buyer's conveyancer to undertake a local search, he will be able to rely on the search in the HIP, and so any delay in obtaining the result of the search will disappear, irrespective of e-conveyancing. (Of course, from the point of view of a client moving house, the overall time from deciding to sell to actually being able to move, will not change at all. The delay in obtaining a search, at present part of the conveyancing process, will, under HIPs, be transferred into a delay before the house can be put on the market.)

Although the Government view is that HIPs are an integral part **5.29** of its reforms of the conveyancing system, they can be regarded as being separate from it and the savings in time (if any) will be achieved irrespective of whether the rest of the transaction is carried out electronically. Of course, one of the many arguments against HIPs is the fact that if we do have e-conveyancing, then the HIP becomes irrelevant. The point here is that if a buyer could obtain the result of local searches quickly, then the provision of that search in the HIP then becomes irrelevant.

But there's the rub; *if* the buyer could obtain the result of the search quickly. There are some 410 Metropolitan, City, Unitary and District Councils, Welsh County Councils, County Borough Councils and London Boroughs which provide local searches. At the time of writing 85 per cent of them can accept search requests electronically via one of the NLIS channels—so saving the time of sending an application through the post—but many of them are still unable to supply the results electronically. Those that can, are able to process applications within a few minutes. The old paper application form sent through the post method of making searches can often mean that the results are not received until weeks later. If all local searches could be returned in a matter of minutes, there would be no need for any transaction to suffer any delay over searches, with or without HIPs or the rest of the conveyancing process being carried out electronically. Maybe if the Government had concentrated more efforts on ensuring that all local authorities were able to process local searches completely electronically, time savings would have come about more quickly and be more cost effective.

Of course, there is still a snag here. Every "chain" of **5.30** transactions can only proceed and be completed as quickly as its slowest link. Ignoring any other possible cause of delay, it would only need one old-fashioned conveyancer to insist on undertaking searches in the traditional way for the whole chain to be delayed. This can only be prevented if some form of compulsion could be introduced. This, you might say, would be politically impossible. However, no-one seems to be objecting to the fact that it is proposed to make e-conveyancing compulsory, which will have exactly the same effect. And, if we accept the premise that a chain can only proceed at the pace of its slowest link, then until e-conveyancing itself becomes the only way of transferring the ownership to land, even when e-conveyancing is introduced, the old-fashioned practitioner who refuses to use it will still be able to slow everyone else down.

In conclusion, it can be stated that electronic searches can save much time in a transaction, irrespective whether the remainder of the transaction is to be handled electronically, subject to conveyancers actually making use of the technology.

CONVEYANCING PROBLEMS

5.31   It is difficult to see how e-conveyancing will save time or otherwise facilitate the resolution of conveyancing problems. It is true that the system envisaged will involve the Land Registry being involved at an earlier stage and validating the content of the contract as against details held on the register, but such discrepancies would not normally cause delays in the completion (as opposed to the registration) of the transaction.

As one of the advantages of e-conveyancing, the Land Registry does stress that it will result in the ending of the "registration gap", the time between completion and the buyer actually being entered on the register as Proprietor. This is often several weeks, because of delays in discharging existing mortgages and the need for the buyer to submit a Land Transaction return and pay SDLT. Electronic conveyancing will enable all this to be done at the click of a mouse button and the existence of the notional register will mean that the buyer will appear as proprietor on the day of completion.

5.32   Whom will this actually benefit? Conveyancers will still have to provide the same details to HM Revenue and Customs as now, but it will all have to be done before completion rather than after. Redemption figures will still need to be obtained before completion in the usual way, so no saving of work there. There will be a saving in that there will be no need to make a separate application to the Land Registry to register the transaction, and a removal of the stress of hoping that the SDLT certificate comes through before the priority period on the search expires, so there will be some advantage.

It certainly won't benefit the buyer in any way at all. The buyer's main concern must be taking possession of the house, not when he is registered as proprietor of it. It will not speed up the time between the buyer deciding to buy a house and the time he can actually take possession of it in any way at all. It is by looking at this period of time that a homebuyer will judge the success of the system, not that there is no longer a "registration gap", a gap that exists at the moment but one that he neither knows or cares about.

5.33   One of the other objects of the Land Registration Act ("LRA") 2002 was to ensure that all land in England and Wales was entered on the register within a 10-year period. This, and the abolition of the registration gap, will mean that we have a Register of the ownership of all of the land in England and Wales that is always 100 per cent accurate. The desire for this accuracy, was also one of the reasons behind the disapplying of the

Limitation Act 1980 to registered land under the LRA 2002, so that squatters can only obtain rights over registered land if they become registered as proprietor. One, perhaps paranoid colleague, did manage to link this comprehensive register to Government proposals for identity cards as evidencing the enormous degree of control the Government wishes to have over all aspects of our lives.

CHAIN PROBLEMS

The idea behind the "Chain Matrix" aspect of electronic **5.34** conveyancing is that this will solve the problems of delays somewhere down the chain.

The matrix:

> "will enable conveyancers and the Land Registry to see the progress of all the transactions linked together in a chain. Chains will therefore become more transparent. The conveyancer's task in synchronising exchange and completion dates should be simplified, with any blockage points being immediately identifiable to facilitate enquiries."

But one has to say immediately that identifying where there is a delay in a chain does not, necessarily, facilitate the removal of that delay. Knowing that somewhere down the chain someone has not yet got a mortgage offer will not speed up the process of that person actually obtaining a suitable offer of a loan. Or finding a property to buy, if that is the problem, or indeed, solving whatever problem there might be in that link in the chain. And the information that there is such a delay down the chain can, in any event, be obtained today.

Certainly transparency can only be a good thing—at least in **5.35** principle. But what conveyancers seem to be concerned about is the consequence of this transparency. At the moment where there seems to be a delay in the progress of a transaction, the conveyancer has the other side's conveyancer ringing up to enquire what is happening, the client ringing up and the estate agent ringing up (and telling the client that it is all their conveyancer's fault). Indeed, this frequently happens when there is not a delay! With the "matrix" in place, the Land Registry Chain Manager will also be chasing the conveyancer in charge of the transaction causing the delay—and as the matrix will provide details to all those involved all along the chain, conveyancers and estate agents up and down the chain will also be able to ring up and enquire how long the delay is anticipated to persist. To try and prevent this, the Land Registry have now, following consultation, introduced a facility on the matrix allowing conveyancers to include "notes", e.g. as to why they are not ready to proceed, or when they are expecting to be ready to proceed. The idea is to explain to viewers what the delay is and so prevent a plethora of time-wasting phone calls. Whether it will put off the over-enthusiastic estate agent is another matter! At least it does show that the Land Registry are responsive to feedback from "stakeholders" on this issue.

There are other fears about the chain matrix. Not everybody in a chain wants to proceed at full speed ahead, or to be totally honest about their situation. As Onora O'Neill argued in the 2002 Reith Lectures, "transparency may destroy secrecy, but there is little reason to think that it destroys. . . deception".

5.36   The obligation to complete the matrix is intended to override basic duties of client confidentiality. So the conveyancer will have to complete the matrix even though the client does not wish him to do so. Keeping information obtained from a client confidential has always been one of the fundamental duties of a solicitor. Presumably this is to be overridden in the "public interest", i.e. in the interest of the rest of the people involved in this chain of conveyancing transactions. Looked at objectively, why should a client want to preserve secrecy over the fact that the results of searches had been received or that a mortgage offer had been obtained? Unfortunately, sometimes clients do wish to make a seller or buyer believe that they are more or less ready to proceed than they actually are. A buyer may not want his seller to know that he has not yet found a buyer for his existing property, or that the buyer that had been found has now withdrawn. If the seller knew that, then the seller might seek an alternate buyer and so the buyer might lose the house of his dreams. Reasons why house buyers and sellers do not want to be totally honest with each other will still continue to arise under e-conveyancing. There are two important questions: Should it be public policy to try and prevent such behaviour? And if it should be, will it actually work?

It is not for a humble conveyancer to comment on what should or should not be public policy. Certainly, buyer or seller backing out at the last minute can be the cause of much heartache in conveyancing transactions. If a seller, for example, wants to change his mind and not proceed, why should he not be able to change his mind? He cannot be forced to sell the house. The same would apply to a buyer who decides not to continue with a purchase.

5.37   As to whether it will work, the first question is, perhaps, whether clients are actually going to be made aware of conveyancers' duties in this area, and if so by whom? At the moment, most house buyers are not aware that, for example, the price they paid for the house is a matter of public record and will appear for all to see on the Register. When they are told, (as arguably they should be), then often they are not happy about it. Presumably, it will be necessary for conveyancers to make it clear to clients that the matrix exists and that the conveyancer is under a professional duty to complete it and that the progress of the conveyancing work will be available for everybody else in the chain to see. It will certainly place great pressures on conveyancers who are told by clients of a problem which they do not want the rest of the chain to know about. Some will no doubt turn a deaf ear in some cases. If the conveyancer does not know about something then he cannot put it on the matrix. Some conveyancers will, right at the start of the transaction, warn clients not to tell them about matters they do not want everyone else in the chain to know about. Deception will still be possible.

Let's imagine that we do have a problem with one link in the chain. At the moment conveyancers have clients and estate agents (and the other side) to chase them up in case of delays. Under the new system, the estate agents and conveyancers acting in other stages of the chain will also be able to phone or email, together, of course, with the chain manager. No one has as yet explained whether this Land Registry chain manager will ever have had any practical experience of the day to day working and pressures of a conveyancer's office, the delays that can occur in obtaining mortgage offers, the pressures of other clients who also want their files attending to, etc. Presumably the chain manager will be a civil servant, with a civil servant's mindset on matters. Not a bad thing in itself, but not necessarily helpful in a pressurised commercial environment where many conveyancers find that, due to constant phone calls, the only time they can get any work done is before the office opens.

5.38 In any event, how any of this will encourage a mortgage lender to speed up its procedures to grant a loan, or a client to contact his conveyancer with instructions, remains to be seen. It is perhaps not a coincidence that this chain matrix aspect of e-conveyancing will be trialed at an early stage.

It is, of course, equally fair to say that some conveyancers are not as efficient as others, (or perhaps take on more work than they can efficiently manage), and one frequently does wish that a swift kick could be administered to them in an appropriate place, but unfortunately, the chain matrix system does not seem to be able to deliver this. It remains to be seen whether the ability for others to see where the delay is, will actually solve the problem. Worries have been expressed that some conveyancers may just not update the matrix regularly, not out of any wish to deceive, but just due to pressure of work: "There is enough to do as it is without having this to worry about as well." As this is to be piloted by the Land Registry later this year, we will probably find out very soon how well this will all work, except that those who are involved in the pilot scheme are most likely to be those most enthusiastic about e-conveyancing and will use the system sensibly. Quite what our old-fashioned conveyancers will make of it is another matter!

"EASIER" CONVEYANCING

5.39   The objective as previously stated is to make conveyancing "easier for the general public, conveyancing professionals, and other parties involved in the process". So will it be "easier" for the house buyer or seller? As the consumer (as we must now call clients) has no direct involvement other than instructing a conveyancer to do the work, the only way any change in the system could be "easier" is if it does result in a saving of money or completion being achieved in a shorter time scale. It can be seen that by making use of email for correspondence and sending contracts and transfers for approval, there will indeed be some saving in time. As stated above, the biggest delays are in getting the result of local searches and obtaining mortgage offers, but e-conveyancing will have no effect at all on the latter. It remains to be seen whether the chain matrix will make it easier to synchronise exchange and completion dates in a chain situation.

5.40   Will e-conveyancing be easier for "conveyancing professionals"? Conveyancing will certainly be different, but the basic stages will still remain the same. So contracts will need drafting and approving, searches will need making and the results studied—even with HIPs not all searches will be included in the pack, and the results of those that are will still need considering in the usual way. Contracts will still need exchanging and the exchange on a sale and purchase must be synchronized, along with completion dates. Deposits will still need to be obtained and handed over to sellers, transfers will still need drafting and approving. The only real difference is the way in which all this is done; there will be no paper documents, just a file on the computer. Exchange and completion will take place electronically, as will the signing of the documents. Information will still need submitting to HM Revenue and Customs, and SDLT paid. The only real reduction in the work that has to be done is that no separate application to register the transaction at the Land Registry will be required—the Register will be changed automatically on completion.

Against this saving must be set the fact that although the key documents in the transaction (contract and transfer) will no longer be paper based, and official copies and search results will also be received electronically, and it is inevitable that all these will have to be printed off and hard copies kept on the file. Many people with experience of "paper-less" offices have discovered that they generate more paper, not less! It is not only people who do not trust computers that find it easier to read a document in hard copy rather than on a screen. Also a hard copy will be essential in case the computer system crashes at an inopportune moment, or it is necessary to show a document to the client when he attends the office.

Speaking of clients, not all clients will be able to/want to **5.41** receive the routinely-sent pre-contract report in an electronic version, but will want it sent to them in hard copy. Also, until all clients have their own digital signature, conveyancers will be signing contracts and transfers on their clients' behalf. No conveyancer will want to undertake the responsibility of committing a client to buying a house without clear written authority from the client, and solicitors will be very wary of signing an electronic mortgage on the client's behalf in case they become personally liable. So what better method of ensuring that the client realises the serious of the transaction and that this will be binding upon them and that they will not be able to change their minds, than by getting them to sign the a paper copy of the contract and transfer and mortgage. This will ensure that they understand the details of the transaction and is essential in order to protect a conveyancer from allegations that the client did not appreciate that they would be bound by a particular document.

Will we have the nonsense of a system where everything is done electronically, but all the documents will still have to be printed off and the client will still need to sign a hard copy document before the matter can proceed? One does not have to be a old-fashioned conveyancer to wonder whether it is all going to be worth the bother at the end of the day.

The total amount of work does not seem much different than **5.42** under the present paper based system. There will certainly be as much paper as now and certainly, in the early stages at least, conveyancers will be extremely cautious over the signing of documents.

Conveyancing will be easier for the Land Registry with the automatic changing of the Register, and the introduction of chain managers and matrixes and early stage validation of contracts will give the Land Registry much greater control over the whole conveyancing process. Who is to say, with all the experience gained, whether one day the Land Registry itself will start offering conveyancing services to the general public?

SALES BY AUCTION

We have so far been concentrating exclusively on how **5.43** e-conveyancing will work in the case of a sale by private treaty, but how will sales by auction fit into the idea of e-conveyancing? Remember, the idea is that the Land Registry, at the time of approval of the draft contract, also prepares a notional register, showing how the Register will look after completion. How can this be done in the context of an auction when the identity of the new proprietor will not be known until the fall of the hammer? The idea of a notional register is an essential part of the e-conveyancing process so that the new proprietor can be registered immediately on completion, thus eliminating the "registration gap" that seems to play such a large part in the Land Registry's objectives.

Further, under an ordinary sale, exchange would take place electronically and a notice is automatically entered on the Register to protect this. In an auction sale there is no "exchange"; the contract becomes binding on the fall of the hammer without the need for any writing or signature. How will this be dealt with under e-conveyancing?

5.44   In theory it would be possible for all potential bidders at an auction to make their bids electronically and for the acceptance of the highest bid to be signified in the same way. All the parties involved would be linked to the e-conveyancing service and the auctioneer's indication of the computerised equivalent of the "fall of the hammer" would then take the place of the electronic exchange. This is not as fanciful as it might seem—internet auctions are, of course, commonplace—as it is only the link to the conveyancing service that would really be new. However, this might involve a complete change of culture for many involved in auction sales—the personal attendance auction for land sales still seems as popular as ever—and the prospect of potential bidders turning up at the sale room and sitting at a computer terminal to make their bids is perhaps a long way off yet, but it may come.

Presumably, therefore, assuming that auctions are to continue as now, rules will have to be introduced requiring the buyer's (or the seller's?) conveyancer (or the auctioneer?) to notify the Land Registry within a stated time after the sale so the notional Register can be finalised at that stage. There is no reason why the contract could not be drafted electronically and submitted to the Land Registry for approval in the usual electronic way. A notional register could then be prepared leaving the new proprietor's name blank until after the fall of the hammer. Following the notification of the making of a binding contract, the rest of the transaction could then proceed electronically in the usual way.

5.45   Another possibility is for all potential bidders to be required to notify the Land Registry in advance so that multiple versions of the notional register could be prepared. After notification of the fall of the hammer, the Land Registry could then scrap all but the one including the actual highest bidder. This seems unduly complicated as there could be many potential bidders although in practice many auction sales only have three or four.

If such a suggestion were to be adopted, there is also the restriction on contractual freedom to be borne in mind. How long a notice period would these potential bidders have to give the

Land Registry; 24 hours? A week? Longer? What if a bidder attends the auction without having registered with the Land Registry? Is the seller really going to be happy for this bidder to be excluded, thus potentially reducing the final price? How are potential bidders to be made aware of any need to register? To be fair, this is perhaps not as great a problem as it might be. Most auctioneers already require potential bidders to register with them in advance of the sale. This is in order to obtain banking details prior to the payment of the deposit now that money laundering precautions preclude the traditional method of payment by the handing over of large amounts of cash.

Auction sales have always been subject to special rules in **5.46** English law (e.g. the contract is made on the fall of the hammer without the need for the usual signed writing) and will probably have to continue to be covered by different rules from other transactions under e-conveyancing if they are to be allowed to continue in the traditional way. The Land Registry is aware of the problems in this area and proposes to publish detailed proposals as to how the system might work with regard to auction sales.

CONTRACT RACES

Contract races are not that common—despite much publicity **5.47** over gazumping—but do pose special problems in an e-conveyancing system. The chain matrix has been designed to include the possibility of more than one potential buyer at any stage of the chain. Where there are multiple potential buyers the matrix will clearly show the possibility of alternate chains being established, dependant upon who wins the "race".

Of course, the underlying idea behind the chain matrix is transparency, with the obligation on the conveyancer to complete the matrix overriding normal concepts of client confidentiality. Is this fair in a contract race situation? Will such transparency be seen as beneficial? In the case of two rival buyers for a property each (or their conveyancers) would be able to see how the other was progressing in the "race". Is this a good thing or not? Views on this may differ.

Knowing that one potential buyer had already received an offer **5.48** of finance might spur the other to greater efforts when, without such knowledge, they might have relaxed and lost the property. On the other hand, potential buyer A might realise that potential buyer B is seemingly having problems obtaining finance. Does that give potential buyer A an unfair advantage?

Potential buyer B might also request his conveyancer to "manipulate" the matrix, to give a false impression of his position, perhaps with a view to deterring other potential buyers from staying in the race. Despite rules as to professional duties, everyone knows that some conveyancers may well be tempted to comply with these instructions.

COMMERCIAL TRANSACTIONS

5.49   We have mainly been considering residential transactions as all the publicity does seem to concentrate on the advantages to house sales and purchases. Indeed, the chain matrix is specifically designed for residential transactions as a chain would be unusual in commercial matters, but the system is intended for use in commercial transactions as well. Will it work in a commercial context?

In a single stand-alone sale and purchase, there is no reason to suppose that e-conveyancing would work any less well than in a residential context. There might be more money involved (and a greater loss of interest due to the funds having to be paid into the EFT system the day before actual completion), but the speed of the transaction will certainly be welcomed in a commercial context where speed is often an issue.

5.50   In more complex transactions, however, there may well be problems. In commercial sales there might be a large portfolio of properties involved; maybe a chain of a hundred or more shops. The simple form of contract shown on the Land Registry's e-conveyancing demonstration model would not be suitable for dealing with large numbers of properties, all with different title numbers. Assuming that this can be resolved, the speed in which exchange, completion and registration of a large number of properties can be effected, will be welcomed.

What may slow matters down, though, will be the need to pay the purchase price into the EFT system the day before completion. In a time sensitive transaction, it may just not be possible to complete on the day required—perhaps essential because of tax considerations—where the money has to be paid into the EFT a day earlier. There just might not be enough days to spare for it to be possible to do this. This will not be appreciated by clients.

5.51   There is also the problem, that often in a commercial context, the transfer of the ownership of the properties is part of a much larger deal. The whole deal might be the subject of one contract. Careful thought will need to be given how this (paper-based) contract will tie in with the electronic contract required for e-conveyancing.

There are also confidentiality issues. The notional register showing the potential buyer as proprietor will only be viewable by the parties. But what if the buyer envisages a sub-sale? Will the sub-purchaser be able to view the details of the notional register showing the price paid by its seller? Equally, will the present proprietor be able to see details of the sub-sale notional register? The Land Registry propose that to deal with confidentiality the seller's conveyancer will only have limited access to the notional register, i.e. just to those matters of concern to the seller and that a separate notional register will be established to deal with any sub-sale.

Special consideration will also need to be given to dealing with **5.52** the common practice of a sale and leaseback. The system will need to be able to create a notional register for both the new free-hold and leasehold titles, the freehold title being shown subject to the new lease. At the moment, all the publicity is about sales and purchases being dealt with electronically. Presumably, it is also the intention for the grant of leases to be dealt with in this way also. It remains to be seen how this will be catered for, as often, in a commercial context at least, there is not a prior contract, the parties proceeding immediately to the grant of the lease, often fol-lowing much negotiation. The Land Registry have now (from June 2006) made the used of prescribed clauses in leases mandatory to facilitate e-conveyancing, but when and how will a notional register be prepared? Will the landlord have to submit the draft lease for approval to the Land Registry (as the draft contract has to be) or will the Land Registry only look at the lease when the grant has been completed?

There would also be a practical problem with some transactions where a plan based on the title plan would not be sufficiently detailed enough. Presumably, some form of provision for this will have to be made. Maybe the plan will have to be scanned into the system?

CONCLUSION

So, will e-conveyancing fly or will it "crash and burn", as one **5.53** person at least has predicted. The idea of making use of modern technology must be a sensible one. We know that the aspects of e-conveyancing already in use—NLIS searches, Land Registry Direct, e-lodgment and Electronic Discharges—do work. Conveyancers should certainly be making more use of them than they do at the moment. There is no reason why other aspects of the proposals should not work also.

The great untried aspects of the Land Registry's proposals are the Electronic Funds Transfer system and the Chain Matrix. The Chain Matrix is being piloted later this year, so we may soon see whether it does help in the ever present problem of the chain.

Speaking personally, the writer feels that, whether or not the **5.54** pilot is successful—and pilots can always be made to achieve the result desired by those setting them up—the matrix will not sur-vive. It is not in any way an essential part of e-conveyancing. It will be irrelevant in commercial conveyancing, for example. A conveyancer can vote with his mouse and the Chain Matrix will probably fall rapidly into disuse. It will just become a nuisance. It is an innovative idea to try and solve the problem of the chain, but maybe we will have to accept that the chain problem is insoluble without making bridging finance much more freely (and cheaply) available so as to break the whole idea of a chain of people having to complete and move all on the same day.

The EFT is the key to much of the Land Registry's plans. The fact that it is not really essential to e-conveyancing as such is evidenced by the fact that the 2007 pilot can go ahead without it. This must be sensible as the EFT could be the weakest part of the Land Registry's plans, and also the part not completely within its control, dependent as it is on the clearing banks. The idea of all the payments throughout the chain being made virtually simultaneously is wonderful if it can be made to work reliably.

5.55   Without EFT, the Land Registry's dream of abolishing the registration gap cannot go ahead. Unless existing mortgages can be discharged instantaneously on completion, the buyer cannot be registered. Is it really that important that we should get rid of this registration gap? Are house buyers really attacking the gates of the Land Registry and demanding that the registration gap be abolished? Do any of them actually know or care anything about it? Surely, the most important thing must be to speed up the part of the conveyancing process leading up to the client being able to move into his new home (or business or whatever). What happens after that has never been of any concern to the client.

The EFT scheme is very adventurous and it is good to know that the Land Registry is taking its time before introducing it. As long as it is only introduced when all the necessary systems have been perfected, then it will be a success. If it is introduced too soon and there are problems, conveyancers will lose faith in it and it will have a serious impact on the future prospects for e-conveyancing.

5.56   Then there are the fears over the use of digital signatures. In theory these are more secure than ordinary signatures and it is likely that the general public will accept them. Conveyancers do still have a good reputation for honesty, so there should be few problems in conveyancers being authorised to sign on behalf of the client. Whether the same could be said of other bodies—which do not have the same public confidence—when they start becoming involved in conveyancing, is another matter. There must be serious concerns about the security of the whole system. It is the case that there has been no reported upsurge in fraud in Ontario or New Zealand who having been using electronic systems for some time now, so hopefully none of the nightmares of the scaremongers will come true. However, the system will only be as secure as that of the least security minded conveyancer who is using the system. We will all need to take extra care at all times. It will only take one well publicised fraud to cause great problems.

So, yes, most of the system proposed will work. It may well prove more open to fraud than at present but whether at the end of the day it will actually make conveyancing any easier or quicker is another matter. If it will not, was there any point in spending all this money on it in the first place?

Index

[all references are to paragraph number]